GROWING

One Day at a Time

© 1999 Modus Vivendi Publishing Inc.

Published by:
Modus Vivendi Publishing Inc.
2565, Broadway, Suite 281
New-York, NY 10025

Cover design: Marc Alain
Page layout: Modus Vivendi
Illustrations: Image Club and Marc Alain

ISBN 2-921556-72-3

Collective

GROWING
One Day at a Time

MODUS VIVENDI PUBLISHING INC.

FOREWORD

When I turned 40, I wondered where all the years had gone. I felt that time had sifted through my fingers like sand, while I was busy with something else. Suddenly, my outlook changed. For the first time, I realized that there were more years behind me than ahead of me. But because I know who I am, I felt no sense of panic. My identity isn't based on my body, my material possessions or my career. Beyond all of these things, I am a spiritual being. And this means that this life is just one of many incarnations. I am here for a given amount of time and then I will experience something different. There is no reason to feel anxious about aging and death. Aging and death are phenomena that affect only the body.

I know only one antidote to the feeling that the years are growing shorter: living each moment as intensely and as consciously as possible. Instead of trying to run away, we must be completely present and we must enjoy every single moment.

This book is dedicated to all those who know that life is short, that the body is bound to age and die and that the soul is ageless. Many people maintain a fundamental confusion: they see their bodies age and they are convinced that eventually, they will lose all. But the fundamental being lasts forever. There is another life after this one. There is no need to think that as our bodies grow old, we grow old as well. The soul always remains strong, present, capable and willful. Despite our physical age, we can learn, love and grow. *Growing — One Day at a Time* is a tribute to all those who know that their value goes well beyond their bodies and the world of physical appearances. Further, *Growing — One Day at a Time* is a wonderful little guide for those who want to remain young at heart, who want to continue to create and grow until they take the final breath.

Growing — One Day at a Time is also a collection of daily thoughts, meditations and inspirational statements drawn from three other major publications: *Happiness — One Day at a Time*, *Success — One Day at a Time* and *Love — One Day at a Time*. To a great extent, this latest book in the series is the result of a collective effort that has led to the expression of the reflections of the editors on the Modus Vivendi team. In this case, the theme of Growth evokes our being's expansive nature. We continue to grow despite failures, distress, illness and the passing years. Growing means becoming more mature, more aware, more tenacious, happier, more at peace with ourselves and with others and more humble in the face of our own imperfections and mistakes. Most of all, growing means learning and acting in complete awareness to improve our condition and the condition of those who share our lives.

The Publisher

CROSSING A BOUNDARY

"When I turned 50, I was stricken with a type of panic, a type of anxiety at the thought that I was nearing the end of my life. I could see the spectre of death galloping toward me as my 60th birthday loomed. Most of all, I wondered how the years had gone by so quickly. But after a few months, I began to see that indeed, there was life after 50. I could take stock of my life and I could decide what direction I wanted it to take. For the first time, I could think of myself, my desires and my dreams. Today, at 54, I know how deeply I appreciate the good things in life. I give myself permission to live and to express myself as I choose. I believe that I deserve to live life to the fullest and enjoy each day in peace and tranquility."

— JAKE R.

*W*e should be able to take the time to live, to breathe deeply and to feel the sunshine on our faces. Life goes by quickly. We should enjoy it now.

Today, I take the time to live and to breathe. I deserve to spoil myself and to make myself happy. I have worked hard and I continue to make a contribution. But I can also enjoy the fruits of my efforts.

BEING YOURSELF

"I can be myself at all times and under all circumstances. The people around me and those who like me are always very happy to see who I really am. Being myself requires no special effort. Being myself is being spontaneous, expressing myself fully, not holding back. When I am myself, I can experience people and things directly. I can be truly present."

— ANONYMOUS

*T*here comes a time in each of our lives when we can't help but be ourselves. No more pretending, no more facades, no more false appearances! We can express ourselves freely and show ourselves to be the individuals we truly are. Some people may be surprised or even shocked, but our true self must come to the surface.

Today, I give myself permission to be myself at all times and under all circumstances. I have no more time to waste by pretending or by building a facade. I hope that those who share my life can live in harmony with me, but I will not compromise my integrity to please anyone, no matter who that person may be.

LONELINESS

"I think that loneliness is my worst enemy. I'm 40 years old and I'm single. At times I spend entire weekends alone at home, reading and fiddling around in my workshop. I'm resigned to living alone, to being alone. But I know that my life could have been different. I have chosen to be alone, but I could have chosen another path."

— PETER Z.

Today, I see that life is filled with opportunities to meet new people. I don't have to be alone, I don't have to be lonely. I can open my life to others.

APPRECIATING THE GOOD TIMES

"As we grow older, the years seem to grow shorter; but the good times can still last just as long."
— JAMES GOULD COZZENS

*W*hen we reach the age of 40 or 50, we begin to wonder where the time has gone. We feel as if the years have rushed by without having really seen them. Our outlook on life changes. For the first time, we realize that there are more years behind us than ahead of us. And time still flies by despite our newfound awareness.

I know only one antidote to the feeling that the years are growing shorter: living each moment as intensely and as consciously as possible. Instead of trying to run away, we must be completely present and we must enjoy every single moment.

Today, I give myself permission to experience every moment with passion and awareness.

YOUNG AT HEART

"I'm trying very hard not to get old. In and of itself, it isn't an easy job. I don't mean advancing in age — growing older is something honorable. I mean growing older in attitude."
— ROBERT R. MCCAMMON

*A*s our physical body ages and as we accumulate painful experiences, we can begin to slow down and lose some of our energy. We see ourselves as old, less capable of facing difficult situations. All we want is a quiet life, undisturbed and problem-free. But such a conservative attitude prevents us from growing and looking at life with excitement and enthusiasm. No matter what, we should strive to stay young at heart.

Today, I know that I'm not 20 anymore, but I know that I'm alive. I can enjoy life and take on new projects. I will use my past experiences and the wisdom the years have given me to make wise choices and to make life an exciting prospect.

WHAT OTHERS THINK

"For a long time, I worried about what other people thought. I wanted to be loved and accepted. I wanted to be part of the group and I wanted to feel that people appreciated me. But now, I know that I have to live life as I choose and I know that I can't decide what others should think. Luckily, people love and respect me just as I am. I don't have to worry about what they think because they accept me unconditionally."

— STEPHANIE P.

Today, I don't worry about what others may think of me. I know that I have to live my own life and choose my own path. I know that I am a good person and that the people who love and respect me will always stand by me.

EXTRAORDINARY GOODNESS

"If we do not love the world we live in, we can always create the world we want through our good and kind acts."
— MELADEE AND HANOCH McCARTY

*W*e all have responsibilities. By fulfilling our responsibilities diligently, we contribute to the good order of things. No one can criticize or blame us for being good fathers, good mothers, efficient workers, reliable colleagues or devoted teachers.

But when we look beyond our responsibilities and when we go beyond this framework to commit spontaneous and random acts of kindness, to some extent, our lives become a way of making an extraordinary contribution to the world.

Today, I know that I can make a difference in this world. I can have a positive and lasting influence on my family, my friends and my colleagues. I can even go beyond what is expected of me and I can contribute to the happiness of a total stranger. And when I do, I make the world we live in a kinder and gentler place.

THE FOUNTAIN OF YOUTH

"Ah! Which of us wouldn't love to drink from the Fountain of Youth and stay eternally young? Perhaps after decades and centuries in this body, I could achieve my ideal life, I could find my ideal mate, visit every beautiful place on earth and conquer the world. But how long would it take before I got tired of such an existence? One life? Two lives? Three lives? After all this time alone with myself, wouldn't I want to leave everything behind and find paradise and my final resting place? On second thought, I don't believe I would drink from the Fountain of Youth — I love this dance of birth and death. It gives me all the time I need to discover who I am and where I am going."

— HAPPINESS — ONE DAY AT A TIME
Collective

Today, I accept the fact that I am here, in this body, for a certain period of time and that then I will leave for another world. I won't be too sad to leave because I know that I have loved and that I have learned important lessons. My consolation is that I am much, much more than a body and my adventure will continue elsewhere, in another form.

MY RELATIONSHIP WITH THE SUPREME BEING

"I've never thought of myself as religious. All the things I was taught about God, Jesus and the Holy Spirit I left behind fairly quickly. But if there is one thing I can be sure of, it is my relationship with the Supreme Being. I consider this relationship to be like the link between two beings of light. I feel that the Supreme Being is my true father. There is an extraordinary degree of affinity between us. I also feel that when I decided to leave my father to look for something different, I was lost. Today, I seek to strengthen my ties with the Supreme Being because I want to come to know him and to feel his love for me."

— JOHN C.

Today, I open my heart and my life to the Supreme Being. Our relationship has not always been tangible, but I know that it exists and I know that it is fundamental. By opening my heart to the Supreme Being, I feel that my life takes on a deeper and more lasting meaning.

THE CHILDREN HAVE GROWN UP

"As I saw my children grow up, I realized that I was getting older. It seems that in the blink of an eye, they grew up and began to choose their own way in life. Today, they are all adults and have their own responsibilities and preoccupations. I love them with all my heart, but I know that they no longer belong to me. I am very happy to have enjoyed the experience of bringing up children, but I wouldn't want to start all over again. I see how much energy, how much devotion it takes and I know that I will experience something different the next time."

— AGNES T.

Today, I accept that there is a beginning, a middle and an end.

WATCHING YOUR WEIGHT

"Before I turned 35, my weight was never a problem. At 35 I weighed exactly the same as I did at 20. I paid no attention to my diet and I practised sports for the fun of it. Then when I hit 35, I started to gain weight. After a few years I was 20 pounds heavier and I didn't feel as good about myself. I didn't want to change my eating habits, I loved to eat. And I was too busy to start an exercise program and stick with it. Over time, I had to change my eating habits and I had to exercise regularly because my weight was out of control and I was afraid of the health problems that might have resulted from my excess pounds."

— JOHN P.

Today, I know that I have to pay attention to my physical well-being. I watch my weight by exercising regularly and by eating well and reasonably. These habits give me energy and protect my health.

WANTING TO STAY YOUNG

*A*s people who belong to the baby boomer generation began to approach 40, marketing experts spread the idea that aging was about to take on a whole new meaning, that it would become fashionable. The truth is, it never did. In reality, baby boomers wanted to stay young. A youth-oriented beauty industry began to thrive. Baby boomers didn't want to retreat from life, from the centre of things. They didn't want to age, they didn't want to pass on the torch. In their own way, they show us that everyone has the right to live life intensely and everyone has the right to be productive until the very last.

Today, I refuse to let myself go. I see that I can stay young at heart throughout my life. I can live a productive and stimulating life until I take my last breath.

TAKING ON A CHALLENGE

"When I was told I had breast cancer, I was completely stunned. I was convinced that my life was over. And even if I did manage to beat the disease and survive, from now on my life would be an emotional desert. After a while, my courage came back and I decided that life was worth living. With the support of my loved ones, I took on the challenge. Today, the cancer is in remission and I am happy to have overcome this trial. I feel that I am stronger and more serene than before and I see that each and every day is precious. I am happy to see that I never lost my courage and sense of humour."

— EVELYNE S.

Clearly, we must remain flexible and open as we grow older. As the years go by, life doesn't get any gentler or any easier. We can take on major challenges regardless of how old we are. There is no need to become rigid in our ways as the years go by. We can use our experience, our knowledge and our wisdom to grow and to continue to discover new things.

Today, I know that I can face life's challenges. I am greater than the problems and the obstacles that life puts on my path.

NOW, I AM FREE

"For a long time I felt trapped inside myself. I think that I had decided not to take any more risks, not to communicate. I surrounded myself with certain specific things and certain specific people to give myself the impression that I wasn't alone, that I was still alive. But as time went by, my life became very dull. So I decided that once again, I would open my heart to life and to others.

As I made my decision, I felt afraid and anxious. But at the same time I felt a surge of energy — the energy of renewal — and a sense of freedom and adventure. Now I know that I can't live completely on my own, without the variety and joy that comes with freedom. Today, I am free!"

— LOUISA T.

Today, I know that I am free. I am open to life's experiences and each day I am willing to take the risks that make me feel alive.

I AM NEVER EXACTLY THE SAME PERSON

"It takes a lot of time and energy not to change — the world around us is in a constant state of transformation. We can use our energy to resist change, or we can ride on its crest and focus our efforts on adapting."

— HEATHER JOHNSON

Today, I know that each minute is new, that each minute brings with it the opportunity for change and renewal. So I can shed my old coat, the same one I put on to protect me from the cold and from abandonment. They say that every cell in our body has the ability to regenerate itself. I know I have the power to be a new person each day.

EMBRACING THE GAME OF LIFE

"As time has gone by, I have set aside a number of preconceived ideas. One of them is thinking that I would work until I was 55 and then I would retire, enjoy life and live on my savings. I look around me and I see that people who have no plans for the future and no passion in their lives never find retirement very exciting. Often they feel that their lives are dull and boring and time seems to drag on endlessly. I have decided to be active and involved until the very end. I want to be part of life and I want to stay young at heart. So I've given up the idea of early retirement. Instead, my focus is on long-term projects and plans."

— JOSH C., AGED 70

Today, I want to plan long-term projects. I am here to create a future and to give meaning to my life. By taking an active part in everyday life, I am aware and present and I can enjoy every single experience.

FEELING GOOD

"Before I turned 40, I never gave a second thought to my health. But when my 40th birthday came along, I started to feel physically vulnerable. I was getting tired faster and it took me longer to recover from setbacks. So I decided to pay more attention to my health. I quit smoking. I started to eat healthier foods and to exercise more often. I realized that an ounce of prevention is worth a pound of cure."

— RACHEL P.

Today, I resolve to maintain and improve my state of health. I know the things that I can do to keep my body healthy and when I do them, I feel good about myself.

A TRIBUTE TO GRANDMOTHERS

Our society has created a faulty image of grandmothers. The typical grandmother always has a smile on her face and always seems to be busy, lovingly cooking special dishes for family members. Grandmothers are supposed to live solely to make their children and grandchildren happy. They work long hours to satisfy others and they never complain.

We know that this idealized image of the doting grandmother is out of date. Every person is different. There are as many kinds of grandmothers as there are grandmothers. In fact, every grandmother is a complex human being and a unique person.

Today, I know that I have the right to live my life as I want to live it. I have my own reality and no one has the right to force a different one on me simply to create the ideal picture. I am unique and I will always be myself.

FOCUSING ON THE POSITIVE

"No matter what happens, we always have a choice: seeing the positive side of things, or seeing the negative side. The more we focus on the positive, the happier we are. Resistance worsens suffering and focusing on the negative side of a situation is resisting that situation."

— SUE PATTON THOELE

Our experience is largely determined by our perceptions. When I focus my attention on the negative side of things, my perceptions have a direct effect on my experience. I cannot be happy if I constantly pay attention only to the negative aspects of life, of my work or of my relationships. I must remember to examine my perceptions before I make a judgement. I must resolve to look at situations from different angles. When I do, I am sure that my perceptions are a true reflection of the situation.

Today, I can look at the positive side of things. I know that I can focus on the positive aspects of each event. I can shut out the kind of thinking that causes anxiety and fear and I can look at the good side of people and situations.

WE NEVER STOP LEARNING

*T*he beauty of life lies in the fact that we never stop learning. Life always has new lessons in store for us. When we are open to new things, life is rich, it becomes a wonderful adventure. When we make the most of our learning experiences, we can see things in a new light, improve our abilities and our skills, achieve better results in our professional and personal lives.

Success and the ability to adapt and to learn are closely linked. When I can learn and adopt new ideas, I can succeed. When I close my mind and my heart, life is closed to me and I experience more and more difficulties and problems.

Today, I am prepared to learn. I know that my success depends on my ability to learn and to adapt. When I am open to the new lessons life can teach me, I am alive and I am happy.

LIGHT

"We cannot learn to be brave and patient if there is no joy in the world."
— HELEN KELLER

*A*t times, we are so burdened by life's problems, we see no light at the end of the tunnel. We feel that life will always be hard, that our problems will always be unresolved. But there is always light at the end of the tunnel, there is always a glimmer of hope, even in the most difficult circumstances. Luckily, life goes on, things change and we set out in new directions. When we are patient and courageous, we can overcome anything.

Today, I am hopeful. Despite the difficulties and problems I encounter, I stay calm because I know that better days are ahead.

I CAN SEE THE OBVIOUS

"There is rest only for those who seek. There is rest only for those who find."
— RAÔUL DUGUAY

Sometimes, I feel upset simply because I didn't take the time to look and see. I imagine all sorts of things based on what I've heard, instead of seeing for myself what the situation really is. How many times have I made myself unhappy by listening instead of looking? Now I see how important it is to look and to see.

Today, I take the time to look and to see what really is. How can I grow if I refuse to open my eyes so that I can see the obvious?

COURAGE

"The only courage we need is the courage that takes us from one minute to the next."
— MIGNON McLAUGHLIN

*W*e can easily be swept away in the rush to the reach the future. All of a sudden, instead of living in the present, we imagine ourselves and where we will be in five, 10 or 20 years. We worry about future consequences without looking at today. Worrying is often the result of our tendency to hurry toward the future, to form a mental picture of all of the consequences that could follow one action or another, one decision or another. Worrying can easily prevent us from taking action and rob us of the joy that life brings us.

Today, I trust myself and my ability to adapt. I can live in the present without giving in to worry and fear.

I Am Master of my Own Destiny

"What we do today, right now, will have a cumulative effect on all of our tomorrows."
— Alexandra Stoddard

*A*bsolutely nothing predisposes an individual to live through a specific experience. There can be no doubt that we are entirely free to choose our own destiny. Only our decisions, our intentions, our perseverance and our tenacity are determinant in the achievement of our goals. We alone can improve our fate. We also can predict our future. Our decisions will determine the unfolding and the ultimate quality of our lives.

Today, I know that I am the master of my own destiny. My decisions and my intentions are determinant. I can accept advice from others, but in the final analysis, I am the person who decides.

THE STORY OF LOUISE

"I have always loved to write. I write naturally, like an artist paints a picture or like a shoe-maker repairs a shoe. Not long after I get up in the morning, I sit down to write. I have written several children's books and a host of novels. I have met with several publishers, but I've never seen my work in print. I'm 55 now and none of my manuscripts has ever been published. Despite the rejection and indifference I have had to deal with in the course of my career as a writer, I continue to write and my work brings me a great deal of joy and personal satisfaction. I'm convinced that there will be a happy ending to all of my effort."

— LOUISE H.

Today, I accept the challenge of doing what I love to do. I know that by doing what I love, I am being loyal to my true self. I want to succeed and I want to grow, but I must respect my fundamental being.

SALT WATER

"The remedy to all ills is salt water — sweat, tears or the sea."

— ISAK DINESEN

*W*e sometimes look very far away for a solution to our problems. We can even go so far that we complicate the situation even further and the problems become virtually unsolvable. Often, the solution is right before us: a little more rest, a little more work, a little more personal discipline. Often, small adjustments that are chosen wisely can make a world of difference in the quality of life we enjoy and in the process we undertake to solve our problems.

Today, rather than wasting my time wondering about the causes underlying my problems, I resolve to make the small adjustments needed to improve my life.

CHANGE

"Modern psychology has given us a whole series of useless concepts. These false notions are based on the idea that Man is an animal and that because the human brain is more developed, it generates a variety of phenomena: personality, emotion, identity, perceptions. Unfortunately, modern psychology has had such a strong influence on the average person's way of thinking that society is in a state of complete confusion. A human is not an animal. Every human has a soul."

— ALBERT DELENCLOS

*S*ome people claim that we can change, undergo a transformation and learn to live differently. Others believe that once formed, the personality cannot truly change. There is some truth to both viewpoints. Essentially, personality, identity, behavior, values, attitudes and choices are the result of our learning, our culture and our temperament. All of these things can change. But the fundamental being, the spiritual and true being, does not change — it simply is. Change lies in the progressive or sudden discovery of our true being.

Today, I embrace my true being and I set aside all things that do not reflect the real me.

FINDING EQUILIBRIUM AND HARMONY

"Be it physical or emotional, most of our pain and suffering stems from a lack of inner harmony. When we are sick, our immune system works actively to reestablish equilibrium within our bodies. In the same way, when we are frustrated, our emotions seek to reestablish harmony."
— SUE PATTON THOELE

*W*e all seek equilibrium and harmony. Sometimes life can be a stormy experience, filled with upheavals and unexpected setbacks. At times, recovering from a failure can be easy, at others it can be hard. However, we can be assured that our being naturally tends to see equilibrium and harmony. Sooner or later, equilibrium returns.

Today, I know that I will find equilibrium in my life. I may experience upheaval for a time, but eventually, harmony will return.

THE LIGHT OF LOVE

"For a lamp to keep burning, we need to add oil."
— MOTHER TERESA

*A*s parents, we can easily yield to the temptation of always giving. We think of our children, our partner, our parents, our in-laws, our employer and our colleagues. But we should remember to recharge our own batteries. We can set aside our own needs for a time. But sooner or later, we have to take care of ourselves. We need to develop a system by which we can think of ourselves and help our loved ones understand that all of us have the right to do the things that bring us pleasure.

Today, I know that I am not abandoning my responsibilities as a parent or a spouse when I fulfill my own needs. When I do the things that bring me pleasure, I can bring new energy to the things I have to do and I can contribute to my family's harmony.

NATURAL HEALING

"We long believed that we were powerless in the face of illness. A sick or injured individual supposedly had no other choice but to place his fate in the hands of doctors. Research has shown that a patient has much more control over healing than was previously thought. Our attitudes, our convictions and our emotions have an influence on the recovery process. We must question the outdated attitude that would have us abdicate our responsibility for our own health and our tendency to place it in someone else's hands."

— SUE PATTON THOELE

More and more people are realizing that they must take responsibility for their own health and that if they fall ill, they must take an active part in their recovery. Modern medical science is very far from understanding the fundamental nature of the human being. Often, we ourselves are the source of our illnesses; as a result, we are also the source of our recovery.

Today, I know that I am responsible for my health. If I am sick, I can play an active role in my recovery.

UNIVERSAL LIFE

A vital force moves within every creature living on earth. An energy lives within each thing, each molecule, each atom in this world. Nothing in this universe is perfectly static. All is movement, all is progression or regression. I may try to close my eyes to truth that all things undergo perpetual change. Even rocks become sand and sand becomes dust travelling on the winds. Stars are born and stars die. I too am filled with the same vital energy — it moves me and it makes me grow.

Today, I know that I am part of the universe. I am alive and I undergo constant change. Each day, I move, I change and I grow.

GENTLENESS

"I believe that humanity will not only last, it will prevail. Man is immortal, not because of all creatures he is the only one with an indefatigable voice, but because he has a soul, a spirit capable of goodness and compassion."

— WILLIAM FAULKNER

G entleness will always be more powerful, more penetrating than brute force. Just as water shows its force in the fact that it has no resistance but can still grind stone into sand, the greatest victories are won with gentleness. Gentleness lets me counter and eliminate all resistance. When I am gentle, I bring things and individuals closer to me and I touch them deeply.

Today, I pay tribute to gentleness. I lay down any arms and I adopt gentleness and kindness as my only intent.

PERSONAL DISCIPLINE

*I*n life, most accomplishments are the result of personal discipline. It takes a great deal of personal discipline to raise a family, to build savings, to keep a job and to move up through a company, to stay fit and healthy, to build lasting relationships. Everything that is worthwhile, all of the major achievements in our lives, are the result of our intentions and our personal discipline.

When personal discipline is lacking in an area of our lives, the result is confusion and constant highs and lows. Without personal discipline, we cannot give shape or direction to our wants. Without personal discipline, we are vulnerable and fickle.

Today, I bring personal discipline to all of the important areas of my life. By respecting my commitments to myself and by persevering along the path I have chosen to take, I know that I can be happier.

A WHOLE NEW DAY

*E*ach day brings new possibilities and opportunities. We can choose to follow our usual routine and to honour our commitments. However, we can also do or say something completely new. We can choose to give ourselves a small gift. We can decide to bring flowers to our partner or to a friend. We can compliment someone to bring something positive to the day.

Today, I take the opportunity to do or say something new. I see this new day as a flower blossoming before my eyes.

SEEING BEYOND A FAILURE

"When my relationship with Lara came to an end, I thought my life was over. I had invested so much energy and so much of myself in our relationship! My personal esteem suffered a setback. For several months, life seemed meaningless to me, I was lost. Little by little, I began to build a new life and the pain began to fade away. When I met Nathalie, I told her I wasn't ready to open my heart to a new love. She was patient with me. With Nathalie, I learned how to love and how to let myself be loved. Nathalie wanted to rekindle my desire to be part of a loving and intimate relationship. She helped me accept the failure of my previous relationship."

— ROBERT W.

Behind every "no", there is a "yes". Behind every "failure", there is a "success". We can learn much more from our failures than we can from our successes. Behind every failure are the things we have failed to learn, the things we have refused to face or accept, the things we do not want to see or hear. When I embrace failure and when I am willing to listen to the secrets it can reveal to me, I am open to growth and to learning.

Today, I know that, eventually, failure leads to success.

REAL LIFE

*W*hen we look at the world we live in, we see that very few people manage to rise above the day-to-day struggle to survive. Most people on this planet live in poverty or under violent and autocratic political regimes. The economic and political conditions on this planet are very harsh and leave little hope for humanity. But still, some individuals rise above the simple quest for survival. They manage to see the true nature of things and beings. They manage to build something that contributes to our collective well-being. The fate of our planet is in our hands.

Today, I thank Heaven for the privilege of living in a democratic society that lets me act and think freely. I know that this privilege entails a responsibility: spreading Good.

THE LIGHT OF DISCERNMENT

*D*iscernment, the ability to make sound and clear judgements, is vital to personal development and spiritual growth. How can I tell the difference between Good and Evil without discernment? How can I see the truth in events without the piercing light of discernment? How can I surround myself with loving and devoted people without discernment? Discernment is something I can develop. When I listen and when I am receptive to the messages that come from my inner self, I can choose and act with discernment. Sometimes I have to pause, say a prayer or meditate before I can awaken to my discernment. But taking the time to listen to my discernment is always worthwhile. My discernment is a powerful asset and I can use it to make fair and enlightened choices.

Today, I know that I have a very deep inner knowledge. Discernment is the result of this knowledge. Today, I will listen to my inner wisdom and I will use the power of discernment when I make choices or decisions.

BEING PERCEPTIVE

"When I realized that I had to have a drink as soon as I got home from work and when one drink became two or three, I realized that I had a problem. I couldn't go through a day without drinking, without using alcohol to block out the pain and the stress I felt. I began to see that alcohol was affecting my mood, my productivity at work and my relationships in general."

— PHILIP P.

*W*ithout our realizing it, some activities and some relationships rob us of our power of perceptiveness. When we are perceptive, we see things clearly and we make enlightened decisions. Without acting on perceptiveness, we run the risk of making bad decisions that can lead to failures and accidents. We know that drugs, the excessive consumption of alcohol, gambling and compulsive sexual behavior can hinder or even destroy our perceptiveness. Compulsions can lead us into a dangerous world of excess, false hopes and weakness. To avoid the disastrous consequences of these forms of excess, we must use common sense and above all else, personal discipline.

Today, I see how important it is to be perceptive. By avoiding the pitfall of compulsion, I protect my happiness and I enjoy a better quality of life

LIFE AFTER LIFE

"When Jeanne passed away, it took me a long time to get over my loss. I couldn't accept the fact that she had gone before me. I wanted to die, in the hope that we would be reunited somewhere in the hereafter. I felt so alone and lonely. Life was colorless. This is when I realized how this woman was actually a part of me. I felt empty and I could see her everywhere I looked. About one month after her death, I dreamt of her. She told me that she was happy and that she would always be close to me. I woke up and I could feel her presence in the room. I told her how much I loved her and how much I missed her."

— MARK-ANDREW H.

*D*eep inside, we know that our material lives are not an end in and of themselves. We are souls that borrow a physical body for a given time. We go through an earthly experience and we form ties with others. These ties go beyond the material world. When we give ourselves genuinely to our love relationship, we come into contact with our partner's authentic being and we cross oceans of time and light.

Today, I realize that I am an integral part of my relationship with my partner.

THE ROAD TO LOVE

"The road to love is filled with pitfalls. It isn't a four-lane highway that we can sail along while the surrounding scenery goes by in a blur. It's a small country road that runs along magnificent landscapes; now and again you stop to enjoy a picnic, you're often late in getting to your destination, and at times, you wonder if it was really worthwhile to come this far."

— DAPHNE ROSE KINGMA

*A*t times we feel that some people are lucky to experience problem-free relationships, while others live in pain and fear. Yet every relationship involves a major effort to love. At times, the work is hard; at others, the effort is gradual. Of course, some couples experience major difficulties: lack of communication, conjugal violence, dependence and drug and alcohol abuse. Making the effort to love is harder and more demanding under these kinds of circumstances than it is when the relationship is balanced. But within a relationship, all is possible. Relationships are places for love, acceptance and healing. Together, we can overcome any and all obstacles! Together, we can change the life we share!

Today, I know that my relationship is a work of love.

TRANQUILITY

"Like water that can reflect the sky and the trees only if it is tranquil, the mind can reflect the soul only in a state of tranquility and calm."
— INDRA DEVI

Today, I take the time to relax and to restore my inner tranquility. I know that when I am calm, I see life from a completely different perspective. I am more peaceful and more receptive and I look at things from a positive standpoint.

TAKING ACTION

"My action is my only wealth, my action is my heritage, my action is the womb that gives me life, my action is my race, my action is my refuge."
— BUDDHA

*A*ction lets us materialize our dreams and achieve our objectives. Action is the concrete expression of our existence and it is proof of our passage here on earth. Action paves the way to self-fulfillment. When I take action, I accept my fate. When I take action, I eliminate boredom and the demons of loneliness. When I take action, I find my rightful place in the universe.

Today, I take action because I know that I am the architect of my present and my future.

THE SUPERIOR BEING

"The Greek word agape signifies understanding and redemptive good will towards all men. It is an overflowing love that expects nothing in return. Theologians would say that it is the love of God that governs the hearts of men. When one loves in this way, one loves all men — not for themselves, but because God loves them."
— MARTIN LUTHER KING JR.

*W*hen I choose to develop my superior being, I choose to develop what is noble, generous and magnanimous in me. I say no to the gratification of the moment and I say yes to justice and to beauty. I can be great. I recognize the moment when I rise to a higher level of functioning and when I abandon my need to be right and to win. I recognize the moment when I choose to develop the good in me and when I go beyond my own limitations to achieve greatness. Some situations require that I set aside a particular position or point of view and that I act in a more generous and more noble manner. When I go beyond my limitations in this way, I awaken the superior being within me. I embrace the greatness in my life and I become a very different person.

Today, I choose the Superior Being in me.

SAY WHO YOU ARE

"Many people tend to think that they are the sum of the things that surround them. When they describe themselves, they refer to their physical attributes, their age, their profession, their marital status and the neighborhood they live in. In essence, to describe themselves, they talk about the things that are not them. Deep down, we all know that we are more than a body, an age, the car we drive or the brand of cigarettes we smoke. All these things are peripheral."

— MARC ALLEN

When I speak about myself, I bring up the things that touch me deeply. I like to describe my dreams and my aspirations, I like to talk about my spiritual growth. And because I define myself as an artist and a creator, I also like to talk about creation. I like to develop winning relationships with different kinds of people and I regard them as worthy of love and respect.

Today, I tell others who I truly am.

A LOVE SONG

*S*ome love songs touch us in the depths of our lovers' hearts. Some melodies penetrate the depths of our being. These songs remind us of the love in our lives and the love that remains in our hearts.

Today, I listen to the love songs that move and touch me deeply.

THE POWER OF DREAMS

"Richard and I imagined that we'd retire at 45. We wanted to sail around the world. We cherished our dream for years. When I became pregnant, our dream fell to pieces. Today, we have a beautiful family and we're happy. I love living and dreaming with my man. No matter what happens, we will always be together."

— RACHEL B.

A relationship is a dream shared by two people. Together, we dream of our future, what we want to achieve together. Every couple dreams of an adventure, a satisfying sex life, material comfort. Every couple's dreams include a family, children, personal growth and maturity. A love relationship is two people sharing a dream and sharing a lifetime.

I can tell you how I see our future and you can tell me how you see it. Together, we can imagine a rich and exciting future that reflects who we are, that inspires us and that helps us move forward and grow.

Today, I share my dreams, my aspirations and my goals and I listen to my partner.

LIFE GOES BY SO QUICKLY

*T*here comes a time when we realize that a whole part of our lives has gone by in a flash. We were busy making decisions, doing and saying things, taking stands. But when we look back, we see that events unfolded as they do in dreams. Time went by, the stakes were clear and now we must cope with the consequences. During such periods of turmoil, we feel as if we've been going through life on automatic pilot.

Luckily, when calm is restored, we can analyze the situation more carefully and we can make more definitive decisions.

Today, I take the time to digest recent events. I can take the time I need to reflect.

AWAKENING TO SELF-LOVE

"True self-love is all the more precious because it is rare. Self-love is not selfishness or egoism; rather, it is the ability to create an inner environment favorable to self-improvement."
— SUE PATTON THOELE

*O*ur relationship with ourselves is determinant in achieving happiness. The way we treat ourselves, the way we speak to ourselves, the opportunities we give ourselves, the pleasure and relaxation we grant ourselves are all crucial factors. Many people tend to neglect their own needs and to focus their attention on others.

Today, I see how my relationship with myself is determinant. So I take care of myself. I give myself all the space and all the time I need. I treat myself as if I were my best friend.

THE CHALLENGE OF LIVING AS A COUPLE

"We started to feel a great deal of stress in our relationship when our third child came along. We hadn't planned on having Luke and our other two children, aged 8 and 10, felt ignored and neglected. I didn't want a third child, but at the time abortion was out of the question. Luke was a difficult child who never slept through the night. To make matters worse, he had health problems as well. From one day to the next, life became a hardship and my husband was less and less present. He spent more and more time away from home and I felt truly alone and abandoned. When our relationship was put to the test, I saw this man's true nature."

— JENNIFER C.-D.

A relationship is a project shared by two people. When we decide to raise a family, we agree to take on a very major challenge. One person can raise a family alone, but the task is easier when two people are committed to caring for their children.

Today, I will be present and I will listen to my family's needs.

AGE

One day, you're 10 years old. One day, you're 20. One day, 40. One day, 60. The dance of time brings us to our golden years. There is no means of escape. Time is merciless as it shows us its ruthless face. There will always be people who are younger than us. There will always be some who are more likeable than us. There will always be some who are wiser than us. But not one of them will escape the march of time.

Today, I know that age is part of life. I cannot prevent the inevitable. I choose to focus my efforts on things that can be changed.

CHOOSING

"During the 70s, everyone wanted to live according to their emotions and their need for adventure. With the feminist movement, I was convinced that I had a stronger attraction to women than to men, that I would find more fulfillment in a relationship with another woman. So I left Paul in spite of the fact that we had two small children. I came up with all sorts of good reasons to justify my leaving and to live my feminist experience to the fullest. But after a few years, I realized that living with a woman involves the same challenges and the same problems as living with a man."

— MAUDE

*W*hen I am part of a couple, I have to consider my partner. My choices can have a major impact. My sphere of influence is considerable. I need not feel trapped or unable to act as I choose, but I must be aware of the impact my choice has on my partner. As time goes by, I know what he or she can live with and accept. As time goes by, I can learn to act in the best interests of the relationship we share.

Today, I am aware that my choices have an impact on my partner.

ACCEPTING THE END OF A RELATIONSHIP

"Saying that you can love one person all of your life is like pretending that a candle can burn for as long as you will live."

— L. TOLSTOY

*A*t the start of a love relationship, passions run high and we can only think that our mutual love will last forever. With time, passion fades and ardor cools. We may even begin to feel trapped. We may choose to stay together for the sake of the children or because of what people will think. We can also choose to experience something else.

Today, I know that I can stay and that I can leave. The choice is mine. I refuse to stay in a loveless relationship through guilt or the fear of being alone.

RECOGNIZING GROWTH

*W*e realize that we have grown when the people or events that troubled or saddened us seem to have almost no more effect on us. We can grow beyond pain, loss and rejection. We can rebuild our lives, find new energy and learn to love ourselves again. We know that we have grown because we finally feel that life is worth living and that day-to-day happiness is at our fingertips. And so we persevere, because we know that we have grown.

Today, I know that I have grown. I feel that I am leaving my pain further and further behind. My harmony and my inner joy are stronger with each passing day.

ACCEPTING THE BEAUTY OF OUR FLAWS

"When we give in to comparisons, our self-esteem usually gets a battering. We can always find someone more intelligent, thinner, more creative, prettier and younger. There are empty spaces in all of us, like the empty spaces in Swiss cheese, but each person's empty spaces are in different locations."
— SUE PATTON THOELE

*T*hey say that flaws are what make a person more endearing. I know for sure that sooner or later, each of us must face our own flaws and our own limitations. We cannot hope to have every talent, every type of beauty, every quality. On the other hand, each of us has our own qualities and our own beauty. Each of us has something to offer. And each of us has the ability to improve and to find self-fulfillment. We grow when we seek to grow. We are beautiful when we are true. We are likeable when we let others like us. Each of us has a few things that need improving. But some of us don't know it.

Today, I know that beauty stems from truth.

SPEAKING THE TRUTH

"I realized that I had not been honest with myself. I had convinced myself that my life was going in the right direction. But deep in my heart, I knew that I wasn't happy. Along the way, I compromised my values and I abandoned my dreams. This realization profoundly changed my life. From then on, I began to set aside all that was not me, all that I had adopted to create the appearance of a happy life."

— JEREMY P.

Today, I look into my heart and I ask myself if I am truly happy. I take the time to seek the truth and to let it guide me.

LIVING FOR YOURSELF

I have my reality and you have yours. I have a vision of what my life should be and you have your own vision. I cannot build your life for you and I cannot achieve your dreams for you. You cannot live my life and you cannot overcome failures on my behalf. We can live together, but we will never be a single human being. We will also be two individuals. Our affinities and our desire to share can keep us together. Our will to love and our ability to understand can bring us closer. But I will always be me and you will always be you.

Today, I know that I will always be me.

SMALL VICTORIES

*A*t times, we have to be content with small daily victories: a productive meeting, a satisfied client, a delivery received on time, a job well done. Success is composed of small daily victories and a multitude of gestures and accomplishments. Individuals who want to succeed find nourishment in small victories as they cross the desert to the promised land.

Today, I see that small victories are like pearls along the path that leads to the fulfillment of all my dreams. My small victories nourish me and quench my thirst.

DIVINE LOVE

"Serene light of my soul, brilliant morning burning with a thousand fires, enter my soul and become the day. Love that enlightens and makes divine, bring to me your power, permeate my very being. Remove from my essence all that is individual, free my being to flow into yours. Remove me from the chains of time, surround me with your divine love for all eternity."

— SAINT BRIDGET

Today, I embrace the divine light that nourishes me and that heals my true being.

LIVING AND GROWING IN SIMPLICITY

*I*s it hard to live life simply? In the evening, after dinner, instead of listening to accounts of the world's disasters on the television news, I go for a stroll. In the morning, before scrambling into my car to take on rush-hour traffic, I take a few minutes to enjoy the fresh air and scenery. I take a few minutes to enjoy my surroundings. I look at the trees and the clouds, I listen to the birds singing; I open my eyes and my heart to Nature's beautiful simplicity. In just a very short time, I free my mind of any problems that may be burdening me.

Today, on the road to success, I take the time to stop and smell the roses. I resolve to develop my inner calm by looking at my surroundings and by taking pleasure in the simple things in life. I understand that it is hard to enjoy life genuinely when I feel stressed and rushed. So I take the time to live and to grow in simplicity.

EXPERIENCE

*T*he conclusions, the attitudes and the decisions that result from any given experience are as important as the experience itself. If, after a tumultuous relationship, we were to decide not to love again or not to make a commitment again, we would be refusing to learn from experience.

We can spend a lifetime repeating the same experience over and over again. When we refuse to learn from the past, we are bound to make the same mistakes time and time again. We must learn from experience and we must use our knowledge to live a better and happier life. Experience can be our guide, but only if we choose to listen to its valuable lessons.

Today, I use my experience to improve my life. I can learn from experience and I can put life's important lessons into practice.

TAKING RISKS

"To be happy one must risk unhappiness; to live fully one must risk death and accept its ultimate decision."

— JUDD MARMOR

I can trust myself. I can undertake new projects and build new relationships. I can take risks because I am ready to trust myself.

Today, I allow myself to take risks because I know that I can trust myself.

A CHILD OF THE UNIVERSE

"You are a child of the universe, as are the trees and the stars; you have the right to be here. And whether or not it is clear to you, there is no doubt that the universe is unfolding as it should."
— DESIDERATA

Today, I see that I have a place in this world. I can breathe and I can take the time to live my life. I have often felt rushed and stressed, but now, I know that I have the right to be here, whole and alive.

THE QUALITY OF THE BEING

"What lies behind us and what lies before us are tiny matters compared to what lies within us."
— RALPH WALDO EMERSON

*W*hen all is said and done, it is easy to see that the quality of a human being makes all the difference. You may own a castle, have a prestigious job or be uncommonly beautiful, but all this pales in comparison to the quality of your inner self.

Today, I realize that what is truly important is the person I am deep in my heart.

BEING PART OF LIFE

"Self-fulfillment does not require that we retreat from a world considered to be insensitive or that we engage in the narcissistic contemplation of self. Individuals become persons by embracing life and by contributing to the world around them."

— FRANCINE KLAGSBRUN

Yes, the world can be insensitive and at times, it can be cruel. Yes, the game of life is hard. However, I cannot withdraw from life and I cannot live in my own little world. I must go forward to discover what my life is and what my true destiny is. I must also participate actively in the lives of others to find self-fulfillment and to contribute to the self-fulfillment of others.

Today, I want to set out to explore life. I cannot discover life if I choose to withdraw and to stay alone.

TAKING A STAND

"In life, some things force us to take an uncompromising stand."
— DIETRICH BONHOEFFER

*I*t is impossible to grow if we refuse to take a stand on things that are truly important. For example, if we want to succeed in a career, we must take a stand and work actively in our field to achieve our objectives. If we want an active and satisfying love life, we must invest in it and we must work at developing and consolidating our relationship. Sooner or later, we must take a stand by stating what we truly want and what we are prepared to do to reach our goals.

Today, I take a stand on the things that I consider to be truly important.

LIES

*S*ome people think that they have to lie to protect themselves or to avoid the inevitable. Lying is the human being's worst enemy. Lies perpetuate a reality that we cannot possibly live in. We become prisoners of our own lies, forced to sustain and hide them. In the final analysis, we realize that it would have been much wiser to tell the truth from the start and to face the consequences than to live with the burden of a web of lies.

Today, I tell the truth because I know that I do not have the time, the energy or the luxury to live a lie.

SENSUALITY

"Sensuality lets us express our emotions in a physical form. The body knows, it urges and it teaches in an eloquent and direct manner. When we are both affected in the same way, when physical love gracefully transports us to ecstasy, without the need for words, we are moved to a joining of body and soul, a joining that soothes all hurts and all wounds."

— DAPHNE ROSE KINGMA

Sensuality, touching and physical love belong in a relationship because they are tangible manifestations of a couple's desire for union. Physical love is a captivating activity. Only in a relationship can we make constructive use of the spellbinding forces of physical love. Physical love is the basis and foundation of families and the desire to be together. Some will say that sex and sensuality belong to everyone, to every human context. Therein lies the problem! When physical love loses its real reason for existing, it finds its manifestation in a multitude of perverted and negative forms. Sexuality outside a love relationship leads only to confusion and personal destruction.

Today, I see that sensuality and physical love belong within a committed love relationship.

BEING SPONTANEOUS

"Spontaneity is the quality of being able to do something just because you feel like it at the moment, of trusting your instincts, of taking yourself by surprise and snatching from the clutches of your well-organized routine a bit of unscheduled pleasure."

— RICHARD IANNELLI

*I*n the strictly regimented routine of our day-to-day lives, we often forget how important it is to be spontaneous. Being spontaneous means being open to the magic of the moment and expressing what lies deep within our hearts. At times, we may be afraid of being judged or rejected. As a result, we learn to be cautious and to behave a certain way under certain circumstances. Alas, a life deprived of spontaneity is a life deprived of sunshine!

Today, I allow myself to be spontaneous.

AN EMBARRASSMENT OF CHOICES

*W*hen we are young, an embarrassment of choices lies before us. We can choose any lifestyle we want. We can get involved in any number of different relationships and we can enjoy any number of different experiences. Life is a long series of possibilities. But as the years go by, our choices become more limited. We begin to feel that all bets are laid and moving on from one situation to another gets harder. We never seem to have enough time and experience has taught us that failure is never far away. We drag our past with us and life seems to be an endless succession of inevitable events.

Despite this reality, we should be aware that we always have choices to make. We always have the possibility of choosing. We can change our entire lives and at the same time, we can be aware that changing nothing is also a choice. We have as many possibilities at 50 as we had when we were 20. But at 50, we have to remind ourselves that choosing is a possibility.

Today, I know that I can choose. I focus on my freedom to choose at all times and under all circumstances.

I LOVE BEING HERE, NOW.

"Yesterday is something that doesn't exist. Tomorrow may never come. All that we have is the miracle of the present. Enjoy it. It is a gift."
— MARIE STILKIND

I rejoice in being here, now. I have gone through difficult times, but now I know that I can handle adversity and difficult situations calmly and intelligently. I am in control of my life. I am in control of my fate.

FOREVER YOUNG

"May God bless and keep you always,
May your wishes all come true,
May you always do for others
And let others do for you.
May you build a ladder to the stars
And climb on every rung,
May you stay forever young."

— BOB DYLAN

Today, I feel that I will be forever young.

KNOWING WHAT I WANT

"You have got to know what it is you want, or someone is going to sell you a bill of goods somewhere along the line that can do irreparable damage to your self-esteem, your sense of worth, and your stewardship of the talents that God gave you."

— RICHARD NELSON BOLLES

*W*e can spend a lifetime trying to repair our wrongs, or we can live the life we choose. Defeatists claim that we have no choice but to be satisfied with what life brings us. I say that we should know what we want and do what we have to do to make sure that life brings it to us. We have the choice. We can be victims, or we can be the authors and architects of our own lives. If we choose to be victims, we feel that life is forced on us and that events are beyond our control. If we choose not to be victims, we can be the architects of our own lives. Depending on our choice, we can be the authors of each day we experience in a lifetime. We always have the opportunity to act, to change, to adapt and to accept.

Today, I take the time to ask myself what I really want.

THE BIOCHEMICAL CONTROL OF EMOTIONS

*S*cientists working for major pharmaceutical corporations would have us believe that human emotions are controlled by biochemical reactions that occur in the brain. These same corporations have created major new markets by selling the idea that drugs and medication can influence human behaviour and emotions. Fortunately, most people refuse to believe them! The body contains a soul that lives far beyond human limitations. Emotions are the result of the state of our being — they are not biochemical reactions of the brain.

Today, I am careful of all forms of intervention that restrict my freedom as an individual and that jeopardize my emotional and spiritual life.

BELIEVING IN YOURSELF

"Some humans achieve success because they are deeply convinced that they cannot do otherwise. Success fills their entire being. Not the smallest of chinks is available to let failure seep in. This kind of belief in one's self is similar to autosuggestion. In any circumstance, events unfold as if failure is impossible, as if they were immune to any negative germ whatsoever."

— FRANÇOIS GARAGNON

Succeeding, achieving your objectives, making your dreams come true requires a form of self-confidence and belief in yourself. The belief that you have the means and the inner strength to reach your goals. In the adventure of life, we must learn to rely on ourselves. An attitude that excludes the possibility of failure or giving up is an invaluable asset. We must develop an unshakable confidence and trust in ourselves and we must know that we can achieve our objectives no matter what. The only possibility is to believe in ourselves and to know that all of our objectives are attainable.

Today, I set aside doubt and I adopt an attitude of self-confidence and belief in myself. I know that I can succeed.

SETTING FLEXIBLE STANDARDS

"When nobody around you seems to measure up, it's time to check your yardstick."
— BILL LEMLEY

*E*ach person has challenges to take on and limitations to surmount. We can choose to judge the people around us or we can try to understand them, to accept them, and to help them.

Today, I will try to be more conciliatory and I will try to be more understanding of the people who share my life. If I persist in judging and criticizing others, I will live an isolated and lonely life.

GET MOVING

"The body is home to our soul. Take care of your body lest it fall to rack and ruin."
— PHILO JADAEUS

I nactivity is the source of many evils. When we move, we stay fit and we maintain a healthy energy level. By walking one or two miles a day, I help myself stay healthy and I help keep myself in a positive frame of mind.

Today, I resolve to get moving! I may not need an athlete's exercise program, but I can move a bit each day and I can enjoy activities that keep me fit and healthy.

MY PERSONAL WORK OF ART

"No one should consider themselves divine to the point of being incapable, on occasion, of improving the creatures they are."
— LUDWIG VAN BEETHOVEN

*O*ur lives resemble works of art. We can create a beautiful life, in much the same way as we can paint a picture, shape a sculpture or compose a song. Our lives are composed of many elements. When they are combined, these elements create harmony or cacophony. We choose the elements that make up our lives. We can add or subtract elements. We can adjust and refine our actions to create a beautiful life.

Today, I see my life as a work of art in progress. As the creative talent that shapes my life, I combine and rearrange its elements to achieve harmony.

THE LIGHT WITHIN

"What we create within ourselves always reflects our exterior. Such is the law of the universe."
— SHAKTI GAWAN

*W*e live in a world of paradox. Our main focus is appearance: we look at an individual's age and physical condition, we look at how opulent his or her home is, how prestigious his or her car happens to be. In reality, these factors are very unimportant. At most, they indicate that a person has succeeded on the material level or is in top physical condition (neither of which is bad or negative in and of itself). However, if we have material wealth and physical beauty, but are not truly happy or truly satisfied, we exist in an inferior state of being.

Today, I resolve to invest time and effort in my awareness and awakening and in my growth as a spiritual being. I know that I am a truly valuable and worthwhile being.

WAITING FOR THE RIGHT TIME

"Who of us is mature enough for offspring before the offspring themselves arrive? The value of marriage is not that adults produce children but that children produce adults."

— PETER DE VRIES

*S*ome people rush into a project without a moment's thought. Others spend a lifetime waiting for just the right moment, willing to miss the boat for fear of experiencing failure. Between these two extremes, we can all find a happy medium. We can realize that success is not assured, while being fully prepared to do all we can to achieve the goals we have set for ourselves.

Today, I take action because I know that I have the intelligence and the ability to succeed. I refuse to wait indefinitely for the right time to act. I refuse to be afraid of failing.

THE LIFE AROUND US

"I love gardening. I love watching flowers and trees as they bloom and grow. I am always amazed to see a plant grow to maturity and I am grateful that it happens to be in my garden. I see my garden as a miniature ecosystem that is home to a multitude of life forms. Plants, insects, birds, water, the sun and the heat dance about and are an endless source of fascination for me."

— THERESA D.-L.

Today, I feel the life that is within me and around me. Right now, I can begin preparing for spring by sowing the seeds that will bloom in my garden.

A SMALL PARTICLE OF DIVINITY

"Forgiving is seeing the person who has hurt you in an entirely different way. Through the eyes of charity and love. Forgiving someone is hard, but it can change your life. Forgiveness brings new life to a relationship and changes the chemistry between two people — from bitterness to kindness."

— DAPHNE ROSE KINGMA

*W*e can learn to forgive, for in forgiveness, there is a particle of the divine. Forgiveness is a noble gesture. It is also a sign of greatness, since it gives us the capacity to rise above rancor, anger and at times, our own pride, to choose the way of compassion. Forgiving may be difficult, but when the emotion of the moment dies down, we must resolve to forgive, if only to focus our attention and our energy on other, more positive things in our lives. Anger is never a good counsellor and bitterness can never be a positive influence.

Today, I forgive because I know the price there is to pay when I refuse to forgive. I want to set myself free from past hurts, and so I forgive those who have hurt me and I forgive myself for mistakes I have made in the past.

SPRING IS NEAR

*M*arch can be a particularly hard month. Snow and cold weather seem to last forever and the days are still too short. But we hear spring's small voice, whispering that more clement days are just ahead. Here and there, we can see small signs that winter is retreating and that better and more enjoyable days are just around the corner.

Today, I feel that spring is near. And with spring, there comes the energy and the hope of renewal.

TAKING ACTION

"The last time I met Mary, I hadn't seen her for years. She had aged. There was no light in her eyes any more. I took a few seconds to ask her how things were. In spite of what she said, I had a feeling that her life was not going well. She seemed worried and tired. I talked briefly about what I was doing and then we parted, wishing each other good luck. About a year later, a friend told me that Mary had committed suicide. I was shocked. I had the feeling that I could have done something when we last met. I was very sad at the thought that I would never see her again."

— MARC A.

*A*t times, someone who shares our lives cries out for help. We must learn to see the signs and to listen to messages of distress, to cries for help. We can do something positive and effective only if we are capable of seeing and listening.

Today, I resolve to listen to others.

ACCEPTING OURSELVES UNRESERVEDLY

"Little by little, I must accept myself as I am — with no secrets, no disguises, no falseness and no rejection of any facet of myself — and with no judgement, no condemnation or denigration of any facet of myself."

— ANONYMOUS

*T*here comes a time in our lives when we can no longer live solely for others or for the approval of others. There comes a time when we understand that we must accept ourselves as we are if we are to grow. When we accept ourselves, we can begin to learn to live in perfect harmony with our inner being.

Today, I know that I am a valuable and worthwhile person. I can love myself. I can give myself the permission to live, to laugh and to have fun. I can do the things that contribute to my well-being and my self-fulfillment. I can learn, I can grow and I can change.

COMPLIMENTS

"Compliments are the verbal food of the soul. They lead to self-love and in a very subtle way, they help create the very essence of each individual. Compliments teach people to see themselves in a different way. Like the layers that oysters form to cover grains of sand, at the same time giving pearls their unique appearance, compliments envelop us in beauty."
— DAPHNE ROSE KINGMA

*E*ach of us needs positive reinforcement in some form. Human beings react negatively to punishment or threats. If we seek to build lasting relationships based on love and mutual respect, we learn to recognize the value of others. Each individual has a unique value. Each individual seeks to make a positive contribution. Compliments are a way to encourage others to develop constructive attitudes and positive behaviour patterns.

Today, I see that compliments are important. When I pay sincere compliments, I show others that they are valuable to me and that they are important to my life.

WORRYING

"We should plan for the future, but we should not worry about it. Planning is a reassuring process; worrying is unnecessary and useless. Planning strengthens; worrying creates victims."

— SUE PATTON THOELE

*W*orrying is an overall, generalized feeling of fear that has no particular focus. Worrying stems from fear of the unknown and a preoccupation with what could happen tomorrow. The only thing I can be completely sure of is that I am here, now. I have had to face difficult situations in the past, and I have survived them. I will be forced to face challenges in the future and I have the resources to take them on. When I realize that I have begun to worry, I tell myself that worrying is useless. Instead of trying to predict future disasters, I choose to deal with the current situation and to keep a positive attitude.

Today, I resolve to set my worries aside and to live in the present.

A NEW LIFE

"New life comes from shedding old skins and pressing through the darkness towards the light. Spring is the season of new beginnings and of growth."

— KAREN KAISER CLARK

A decision can change everything. A step in the right direction can open new horizons that may have been closed. We can decide to live a new life and to begin the process of change, the process that will lead to a whole new life.

Today, I know that I can begin the process of profound change and I know that it will lead me to a new life.

SAYING GOODBYE TO INDIFFERENCE

*T*oday, I can say goodbye to indifference. I can free myself of the negative and harmful influence that indifference has in any life. Today, I can surround myself with people who appreciate me. I can surround myself with interesting and appreciative people who want to learn new things and enjoy new experiences. I want to shed my indifference and I want to live an active life.

Indifference eventually leads to abandonment and apathy, so when I see that I am indifferent, I take my life in a different direction.

Today, I say goodbye to indifference.

SHARED JOY

"Shared joy is double joy, and shared sorrow is half-sorrow."

— SWEDISH PROVERB

Life is made to be shared. We cannot grow alone. We must include others in the process of change, growth and learning. When I include others in my life, it takes on a more meaningful dimension. In addition to sharing my sadness and my joy, I learn to contribute to the joy of others.

Today, I know that I am not an island. I can share my joy and my sadness with the people who share my life, and when I do, my life becomes more meaningful.

THE TRUTH OF THE MOMENT

"If I am unable to find pleasure in washing the dishes or if I want to get the job over with as quickly as I can so that I can sit back down at the table to eat my dessert, I am equally unable to enjoy my dessert! As I pick up my fork, I am thinking about the next task that awaits me and the dessert's texture and taste and all the pleasure it brings fade into the background. I will always be dragged into the future and I will never be capable of enjoying the present."

— THICH NHAT HANTH

*W*e can spend a good part of our lives racing to reach the future, convinced that happiness, success and love are just around the corner. We can feel that life will be better, that we will be happier only once we have achieved one goal or another. We feel that one day, all of the many aspects of our lives will fall into place and then, at last, we will finally begin to live. When we adopt this viewpoint, we are not living in the present. We are less available for others and for the many experiences that life brings us.

Today, I say: "Why do I need to rush to retirement when my real life is here and now?"

MY REAL AGE

"I have the deep conviction that all those who are the same age as me are adults, and that I am simply disguised as one."
— MARGARET ATWOOD

*W*hen we look in a mirror and see how we have aged, we realize that we are mortal. The process of physical aging can be slowed, but it is inevitable. We can easily resign ourselves to the situation, or we can begin to think that life is unfair. Growing old can be hard to accept.

On the other hand, we should remember that true beauty, vitality and youth all come from the heart. Our love for ourselves and for life can permeate and illuminate our faces and can energize our bodies.

Today, I know that the source of my youth and my vitality lies within me. I embrace the light of life and of joy and I refuse to worry about the years and the physical changes that come with them.

AN ETERNAL BEGINNING

"The only thing sadder than an unfinished work of art is a work of art never begun."
— CHRISTINA ROSSETTI

*W*e have the opportunity of living the life we have always wanted for ourselves. We have the opportunity of doing things that will have a lasting effect here on earth. Why wait until tomorrow when we can begin today?

Today, I resolve to take action. I know that now is the right time to make my dreams come true.

LEARNING FROM FAILURE

"Most of our limitations are self-imposed. When we are convinced that we can achieve something, we generally do. But such conviction is more than wishful thinking. Taking one's wants for reality is a passive effort; deep conviction requires that we find a clear path to our goals and that we avoid the stumbling blocks we encounter along the way."

— SUE PATTON THOELE

We must measure ourselves against a realistic objective. We must see things as they truly are and we must learn from the consequences of our actions. Failure is our environment's objective response to our actions. When we fail, we must identify which actions, which behaviour patterns and which factors have contributed to our failure. Failure brings many valuable lessons. We can learn more from failure than we can from success.

Today, I know that I can learn from my mistakes. I refuse to let the prospect of failure prevent me from taking action. I know that I can take action and I know that I can deal with failure.

MATURING

"If aging is sad, maturing is not."
— BRIGITTE BARDOT

*M*odern societies convey harmful notions on aging. Some people consider seniors as a burden, a social problem that should be left to the State. We have convinced ourselves that the world belongs to the young and that mature people have exhausted their abilities and their usefulness. This is extremely unfortunate. In a society filled with throwaway products, the elderly seem to be as easily discarded as cigarette lighters or ballpoint pens.

But society is beginning to change. Despite advances in technology and science, despite the intense promotion of the virtues of youth, mature individuals have a rightful place in society. It is becoming increasingly difficult to set them aside thoughtlessly. They have their own material and financial resources. They control political power. They have extensive academic training. Within a few years, we will witness a true revolution in our perception of age and the aging process.

Today, I realize that I play a key role. I cannot be replaced easily. I look at the younger generation and I know instinctively that it will need me.

CAUTION AND COURAGE

"When caution is everywhere, courage is nowhere."
— HIS EMINENCE CARDINAL MERCIER

A variety of social and financial mechanisms encourage caution. Life insurance, health insurance, savings plans, retirement programs, employment insurance, collective agreements, etc. All these risk-reducing programs are valuable and they contribute to our need for security. However, life requires not only caution, but courage. We need the courage to act, to live and to stand among those who take action to improve society.

Believing that we can accumulate promissory notes throughout our lives and that we can cash them in whenever we may be in need is a completely false notion. Life is not a game. Life is a series of dynamic and exciting experiences that encourage me to take action.

Today, I see life as a series of dynamic and exciting experiences that give me the courage to take action.

A REASSURING RELATIONSHIP

*A*ll of us need a stable framework that enables us to grow emotionally and spiritually. Within this basic form of stability, human beings are overwhelmed with doubt and experience constant anxiety. We must know where we stand, who we share our lives with and we must know that our survival is not jeopardized at every turn. Unfortunately, many people live in fear and insecurity.

Today, I know that I need a form of emotional stability and security. Without this foundation, I cannot grow. And so I seek to create a stable climate of emotional, spiritual and material stability. Without such a climate, I cannot grow.

THE POWER OF MY DECISIONS

"I have realized that there is power in my decisions. I decide to act or not to act, to be or not to be. The world is driven by decisions. The fact that I can make a decision energizes me and boosts my self-esteem. With time, I have realized that I am the author of my own life. I am the person who decides. My decisions are extremely powerful. With the power of my decisions, I can change whatever I want to change, I can build whatever I want to build, I can destroy whatever I want to destroy."

— HAPPINESS — ONE DAY AT A TIME

Today, I decide and I realize that my current environment is the result of the decisions I have taken in the past. When I want to change something, I look at the decisions I have made in the past and I resolve to make new decisions.

REALITY

"Each time I close the door on reality, it comes in through the window."

— ASHLEIGH BRILLIANT

*T*here are two kinds of reality: the inner reality that each of us has and the exterior reality of the material world and other human beings. We must be aware of both types of reality. When I try to run away from my own reality, it finds many different ways of manifesting itself. And when I try to run away from the exterior reality of the world, it always manages to catch up with me.

Today, I know that I cannot run from reality. I have my own inner reality and I cannot deny it and I must be equally aware of the exterior reality of the world I live in.

LAYING BLAME

*W*e are often the authors of our own misfortune. It is easy to hold someone else responsible for our troubles. In circumstances marked by misunderstandings or hurtfulness, we can feel that the other person is responsible. Close relationships make it easy to hold others responsible for a given situation.

But transferring responsibility to someone else's shoulders is wrong and can lead only to guilt and a breakdown in communication. In reality, we are completely responsible for what happens to us.

Today, I have stopped blaming others for my misfortunes and my difficulties. I know that I am responsible for all that happens in my life.

GRADUAL PROGRESS

"Victory is won not in miles but in inches. Win a little now, hold your ground, and later win a little more."

— LOUIS L'AMOUR

*W*e usually think that major accomplishments call for grandiose gestures, major resources and relentless perseverance. In truth, such accomplishments call for sustained work over a long period of time and the ability to establish a clear idea of the results we want to achieve.

When I am deeply saddened, a day without pain and regret is an accomplishment in itself.

Today, I know that victories are won one step at a time.

DARING

"We do not fail to dare because things are difficult. Things are difficult because we fail to dare."
— SENECA

*E*ven if we are aware of the need to act, by constantly putting off a decision, we make the situation even worse for ourselves. The barrier blocking the way to action becomes increasing higher and our objective becomes proportionally unattainable in our eyes.

Today, I resolve to act!

DARING TO DREAM

"If you can dream, you can make your dream come true."

— WALT DISNEY

*D*reaming is imagining a better future. Dreaming is seeing our wishes take a material and concrete form. Dreaming is believing that the possibilities and opportunities available to us go far beyond our current reality. And when we stop dreaming, we stop living and we stop moving forward.

Today, I dare to dream!

I Love the Person I Am

"When we truly love ourselves, when we approve of who we are and when we accept ourselves as we are, life is beautiful. It is as if small miracles occur all around us."

— Louise Hay

We can tell ourselves: "I love who I am and the person I am becoming. I have all the talent and the attributes I need to succeed. I deserve to succeed because I am a valuable person who seeks to do good. I congratulate myself for being the wonderful person that I am."

We can move away from the enemies that destroy our self-love. There are many such enemies and they take many forms: negative comments, individuals who sow confusion and doubt regarding our personal integrity and who choose to build relationships based on dependence. There are many mechanisms that help us reinforce our self-love: work, communication, physical and mental fitness, a willingness to embrace our emotions, the affirmation of our needs and the setting of definite personal limits.

Today, I resolve to move away from the enemies that seek to destroy my self-love.

HOPE

"If we were logical, the future would be bleak indeed. But we are more than logical. We are human beings, and we have faith, and we have hope, and we can work."

— FRANÇOIS GARAGNON

The human condition is particularly astonishing. We invest in a physical body that in truth is not very different from a monkey's. Of course, we are mammals. But we are so much more as well. We share complex communication systems. We use very sophisticated technologies. We have extremely refined perceptions and we are capable of establishing relationships with a spiritual and moral universe. We are privileged beings; we have an undeniable tie with the subtle world of the soul and creation. We must absolutely develop an awareness of the wonderful powers within each of us.

Today, I am aware of the wonderful potential I have to take action. I can act and I can grow because I am so much more than a merely physical entity.

LOOKING BEYOND THE CLOUDS

"Remember that each cloud, as black as it may be, always has a sunny side, resolutely turned toward the open sky."

— W. WEBER

*W*hen we are faced with the loss of a loved one, with a failure or with the fight to survive, we can easily forget that there is a positive side to each and every experience. What does not kill us makes us grow. And what makes us grow makes us better human beings. We can grow each day and each of our experiences can contribute to our growth.

Today, I see the positive side to every experience.

I CAN MOVE BEYOND THE NEED TO SUFFER

"Now, I realize that I have moved beyond the need to suffer. I have realized that suffering has no intrinsic value. I used to associate suffering with change and spiritual growth. So whenever I was suffering, I told myself that the situation was inevitable and that I had to suffer to grow and to attain a higher level of awareness and maturity. But in and of itself, suffering does not make a person better, more spiritual or more honest. Suffering simply makes me a human being who is suffering."

— LOUISE H.

There is a positive aspect to suffering. When we suffer, there is a cause underlying our suffering. Something is wrong with our lives. So in situations of emotional turmoil, we must identify the reasons for our turmoil and we must seek to make the appropriate changes.

Today, I know that no suffering is in vain. I rely on my suffering to make the changes I need to make in my life.

CHANGING HOW WE SEE THE WORLD

"The optimist looks at a rose and sees no thorns. The pessimist looks at the thorns and sees no rose."

— ARAB PROVERB

*O*ur point of view is a determinant factor in the things that happen in our lives. If we are convinced that life is filled with stumbling blocks and that it always will be, there is no doubt that life will indeed be hard. Similarly, if we are convinced that events always unfold as they should, we will always enjoy inner equilibrium and harmony. Life depends on our point of view and our actions are the result of our perceptions.

Today, I examine my perceptions. I see that my perceptions are at the root of my point of view and my actions. When I weigh my perceptions carefully, I can maintain those that are positive and I can reject those that are harmful to my inner peace.

LISTENING TO MY OWN ADVICE

"Believe nothing, oh monks, simply because you are told it. Do not believe what your teacher tells you simply because of your respect for him. But if, after examination and analysis, you judge the principle to be sound, to hold the promise of goodness and well-being for all living beings, then believe in it and let it be your guide."

— BUDDHA

*E*ach and every one of us has opinions. These opinions and viewpoints can be very interesting and can show us the truth. But I have also realized that I must move forward and I must discover things for myself. I must live through my own experiences, I must examine facts myself and I must reach my own conclusions.

Today, I respect the opinions of others but I base my decisions, my values and my life on the truths that I have experienced and tested.

WANTING

"People who have a deep want for something are almost always well served by luck."
— HONORÉ DE BALZAC

*W*anting and intention send a very powerful message to the universe. If we truly want something and if we intend to achieve it, the universe inevitably complies with our request. Such is the way of the universe. It bends and shapes itself to the mold of our basic intentions.

Today, I know beyond the shadow of a doubt that I will achieve my goal.

DISCERNING BEAUTY

"When we are hurt or upset for some reason and when our mind is intent on finding the reason, we should focus our thoughts on beauty. We need discipline and resolve to change the direction of our thinking."

— SUE PATTON THOELE

*T*here is a form of equilibrium in beauty. We can experience this equilibrium by looking at a picturesque landscape, by contemplating a sweet-smelling flower or a colourful bird, by listening to soothing music. Contemplating the beauty that surrounds us is a source of energy and inspiration, it calms us and gives us hope.

Today, I am aware of my environment and I admire the beauty it holds.

SMALL PLEASURES

"Too many people have preconceived ideas about their way of living. In truth, they miss out on the many small pleasures that life can bring."
— CHRISTIANE DUFRESNE

*W*e can hope to get the job of our dreams, the home we covet, a financial windfall the plastic surgery that will make us the envy of all. On the other hand, we can live for today and we can enjoy the people and things around us right now. Living in the present and appreciating the many beautiful things that life brings us does not prevent us from dreaming and imagining a better life. However, if we embrace life at every moment, the road to self-improvement is no longer a hardship, but yet another pleasant and enjoyable experience.

Today, I can rejoice in life and in what the present moment brings me.

I AM HERE TO LOVE AND TO LEARN

"I deeply believe that I am here to love and to learn. Such is the essence of my mission on earth. I know that I can fulfill this fundamental mission in countless ways."

— ED ARIAL

*E*ach day, we must be open to new lessons and to opportunities that help us increase our knowledge and our level of awareness. We can share our knowledge by serving others. We can contribute to the well-being and happiness of the people who share our lives. Although not all of us may be capable of sainthood, we should always remember that we can love and we can learn throughout our lifetimes.

Today, I know that my life has meaning. This feeling stems from my mission: to love and to learn each day.

MY INDIVIDUALITY

"I am a complete, independent and determined spiritual being; therefore, I can also make the following affirmation: I am completely different from all other human beings. I am profoundly individual; I have an innate and deep wisdom that is incontestable and infallible; I have qualities that are mine alone; I have a very special mission as a human being."

— JAMES P.

Today, I recognize and I accept my profound individuality.

ACCOMPLISHING GREAT THINGS

"It takes a great deal of naivety to accomplish great things."

— R. CREVEL

*A*s we grow older, we may come to think that we cannot do much to change our world. This comes as no surprise — we are constantly confronted by indifference and apathy. We hear more talk of failure and tragic events than we do of heroic accomplishments. But each day, small miracles do occur. Some individuals and some groups succeed in surmounting all obstacles and in creating a better world.

Today, I know that I can do good things and I can contribute to building a better world.

AWARENESS

*T*he physical body is designed to perish, but the soul lives on and is linked to its physical body only for a short time. This principle may never be confirmed by scientific theory, but in my heart, I know that my soul goes beyond my physical body. If I am not my body and the outward person I am, then who am I? I am a being of light, of greatness and of infinite good.

My body is a vehicle that I have borrowed for a short while. My body is simply the vessel that carries me through my earthly experience. My body's perceptions (sight, sound, smell, touch, emotions, etc.) are partial and biased and convey only a small part of reality. To make contact and come to know things and individuals in the true sense, I must open my heart and I must refine the perceptions that stem from my soul. Today, I see aging and dying as unimportant because I know that death is not an end, but a new beginning.

Today, I open my eyes, my heart and my mind. Today, I recognize that awareness is divine.

RECOGNIZING THE ESSENTIAL

*I*n our quest for happiness, we agree to make some compromises, and others we refuse. It is a matter of determining what we are prepared to accept without the need to give up the satisfaction of our needs. At times, an opportunity arises and we are free to see that it does not reflect our expectations. However, when we take a closer look, we realize that it can indeed help us meet our needs. We should never reject one particular answer out of hand simply because it does not correspond to the image we have of ourselves.

Rather than a series of compromises, life is an alignment of effective solutions that lead to overall satisfaction.

Today, I accept effective solutions with the knowledge that each opportunity contributes to my happiness.

VIRTUOUS ACTION

"I have learned this: it is not what one does that is wrong, but what one becomes as a consequence of it."

— OSCAR WILDE

*T*here is a superior logic in virtuous attitudes and behaviours, a road that leads directly to serenity, freedom and success. But along the way, we have forgotten or lost sight of the inherent value in virtue. We see in goodness, compassion and kindness something archaic, something that has no place in modern society. But virtue is never misplaced; it paves the way to salvation, divinity and success. Virtuous attitudes and behaviours are tangible manifestations of the true self and around each human being they create an aura of dazzling light.

Today, I recognize that virtue is crucial to my personal growth.

DOING ONE THING AT A TIME

"I have come to realize that it is better to do one thing at a time instead of taking on several activities at once. When you run your own business, it is easy to feel overwhelmed by the work load involved. The prime quality of any good entrepreneur is establishing priorities and doing one thing at a time, as efficiently as possible. Being effective calls for careful attention. It requires focusing one's attention and energy on the task at hand. The best strategy is doing one thing at a time."

— MARC ALLEN

Today, I do one thing at a time. When I do one thing at a time, I can be attentive and I can focus my energy and my effectiveness on the task at hand.

THE WISE OLD FOX

"The young wolf has teeth to defend itself. The old fox has the wisdom not to get caught."
— FRANÇOIS GARAGNON

*W*hen we are young, it is easier to recover from life's difficulties. Failure is much harder to handle when we are older. On the other hand, the experience that comes to us as the years go by is a major asset; we have a better understanding of the rules of the game and we have a greater ability to predict the outcome of our actions.

Today, to avoid life's pitfalls, I rely on the experience and the wisdom that I have accumulated over the years.

OUR FEELINGS

*W*e can embrace our feelings. Eventually, the feelings we refuse or reject are expressed in one form or another. We can let our feelings rise to the surface and when they do, we can express them in a positive and constructive way. Feelings are a manifestation of our emotions. The word "emotion" contains the word "motion". When we try to hold back or stop the natural movement of our emotions, we imprison their energy within us.

Today, I let my feelings rise to the surface and I let myself express them in a positive and constructive way.

Building a Future

"We do not suffer the future, we build it."
— G. Bernanos

*W*e can see ourselves as the architects of our lives, or as the victims of circumstances. No one can tell us how our lives will unfold; each life is a creative experience that is shaped on a daily basis. The experiences we encounter, the conclusions we reach and the considerations they involve are determinant. Despite what clairvoyants and astrologers may claim, the stakes are never set in advance. Our only fate is the fate that we determine for ourselves.

Today, I see that I am the author of my own fate. I am the only person who can decide what my life will be like.

A WINNING ATTITUDE

*A*dopting a winning attitude is very important. A positive attitude paves the way to success, it helps us take on projects with determination and energy. Winners want to win. Winners know that in the long run, with work and resolve, they will win. Winners never contemplate the possibility of failure. They may lose some battles, but they use the experience to increase their wisdom and their skills. Winners use each of life's lessons to win.

Today, I adopt a winning attitude. I know that I can be a winner and that eventually, my efforts will be rewarded. I look at the road ahead and I move forward. I use my inspiration and my talents to succeed.

STANDING ON MY OWN TWO FEET

"I take pleasure in standing on my own feet. I've always known that to be truly free and happy, I must be independent and self-reliant. At times I've been afraid and I've thought that I might not be able to meet my own needs, but now I know that no other person can support and love me as much as I support and love myself.

"I've always known that by working, I can protect my independence and my dignity. I don't wait for someone else to tell me what to do and how to do it. I am a competent and productive person. By working, I find self-fulfillment!"
— SUCCESS — ONE DAY AT A TIME

Today, I take pleasure in standing on my own two feet. I know that I can be free only if I am self-sufficient and self-determined.

SLOWLY BUT SURELY

"Do not fear moving forward slowly, fear only stopping."

— CHINESE PROVERB

The greatest victories are won with patience and perseverance. We move forward one step at a time and we win small victories all along the way. Major accomplishments require hard work done over the long term, fuelled by the conviction that one day, we will achieve our final objective. In a society focused on easy credit and quick consumption, all too often we forget that the greatest victories are the fruit of effort that is sustained over a long period of time.

Today, I know that the greatest victories are the result of patience and perseverance.

THE MAGIC OF SILENCE

*T*here is a type of magic in silence, in the absence of sound and noise. Silence is alive and active. Silence is a window that shows us what is possible, that shows us what goes unseen in the cacophony of everyday life. Our heart and our soul seek silence to manifest themselves, to speak to us. In moments of tranquility and silence, when we are in contact with our inner calm and our courage, we can feel ourselves grow to take our rightful place in the universe.

Today, I set aside a few minutes to enjoy silence. I use silence to restore my inner peace and to listen to myself. I can use silence to bring me closer to God.

WALKING AND THINKING

"We have to walk and think, not sit and think."
— ARMENIAN PROVERB

*M*odern life can be very sedentary. For the first time in history, humans can live an almost entirely sedentary life. Cars, escalators, elevators, subways and other means of transportation bring us from place to place and all the while, we are seated. But the soul is master of the body. When the soul commands, the body must obey. The relationship between body and soul is refined, filled with subtlety and rewards. When we walk, something happens between our soul and our body. Walking is a form of creative synergy.

Today, I walk because I know that walking has a magical power.

THE BOUNDARIES OF THE SOUL

"There is a distance, a space between you and me. I am me and you are you. I am a complete, separate and independent being. You are a complete, separate and independent being. I have my point of view, my opinions, my wants and my own realities and they are different from yours. I have the right to be who I am, to think my own thoughts and to experience my own emotions and you have the same right. I respect your right to individuality and I ask that you respect mine. You have a deep inner wisdom and I have mine."

— MARC ALLEN

*L*ove and sharing are possible only in a climate of mutual respect and affirmation of mutual boundaries. All of us surround ourselves with a safe space that makes it possible to live without fear or confusion.

Today, I recognize that there is a difference between who I am and who you are. I respect your space and your individuality and I ask that you respect mine.

FINANCIAL SECURITY

"My mother has always been independent. She has always worked and she has always shouldered her own responsibilities reliably and honorably. As a businesswoman, she has worked closely with banks to finance her commercial activities. But she has always known that bankers are people who lend you an umbrella when the sun is shining and take it back when the rain starts."

— MARY P.

*W*e must realize that we are all responsible for our own financial security. Of course, governments can provide some forms of assistance, but which of us is content to live off society? To establish financial security, we must work, save and build a diversified investment portfolio. Financial security and personal independence go hand in hand. How can we be free, happy and self-reliant without a stable source of income to ensure our subsistence and to concretize our objectives?

Today, I take my finances in hand and build my own financial security.

HUMAN RELATIONS

"The only true luxury is the luxury of human relations."
— ANTOINE DE SAINT-EXUPÉRY

*H*uman relations are the only truly worthwhile thing in this entire world. I may accumulate endless material wealth, I may be president of the world's most impressive corporation, I may be the head of the world's most prestigious university, but without human relations, my life will be meaningless. As my life draws to an end, my greatest reward will be the ability to say that during my time here on earth, I have contributed to the happiness of others.

Today, I invest in human relations. I see that they are the greatest wealth in life.

THE SPIRITUAL HOME

"The natural world is a spiritual house... Man walks there through forests of physical things that are also spiritual things, that watch him with affectionate looks."

— CHARLES BAUDELAIRE

Today, I take the time to walk through the woods to be among living things and to draw new energy from them.

THE HURTS I HAVE SUFFERED

*I*t is easy to give in to hatred when someone hurts us. But hate is a negative emotion that leads nowhere. Within ourselves, we must build a climate that encourages forgiveness, compassion and generosity.

Today, I know that I can wipe the slate clean and I can forgive the people who have hurt me. Forgiveness frees me from the clutches of bitterness and hatred. Perhaps I cannot forget; however, I can turn my back on anger and bitterness and I can tell myself that what is past, is past. I can use these experiences to guide me in my future relationships. In the end, I am here on earth to learn.

GREATNESS

*I*t is not enough to accept responsibility only for the things that affect us directly; we must also accept responsibility for the world we live in. When we ensure our own survival, act appropriately with others and strive to achieve personal growth, we are already on the right path. But as we move forward and as we grow, we must extend the sphere of our personal responsibility. We are the co-creators of our communities, our cities, our society and our planet. It is erroneous and dangerous to believe that our actions and our attitudes have no influence on others and the way in which society develops. All that exists is of direct or indirect concern to us.

Today, I accept a larger part of responsibility for the world I live in and I seek to contribute to its well-being.

SELF-AFFIRMATION

*W*hile it is important to be kind and courteous in all of our interactions with others, at times we may overlook the importance of self-affirmation. When we affirm our needs, we teach others to respect us. Self-affirmation is a means of demanding respect for our rights and our wishes. Self-affirmation is an expression of our point of view, our needs and our demands. How can we be happy if we fail to affirm who we are? If we don't, we will be forced to make endless concessions to the demands and the will of others.

Today, I affirm who I am.

PRAYER

"We cannot approach prayer as we do everything else in our push-button, instant society. There are no prayer pills or enlightenment capsules."
— JANIE GUSTAFSON

*I*n its most basic form, prayer is communication with the world beyond our world and with the Supreme Being. Despite the weakened presence of organized religions in the Western world, most people continue to believe in God. It is equally surprising to see that when they experience emotional distress, many people turn to prayer, to a desire to grow closer to the Supreme Being.

But we need not wait until our lives are in turmoil to establish a closer relationship with the Supreme Being. Even when our lives are running smoothly, this process can be extremely beneficial.

Today, I pray. I pray to establish contact with the Supreme Being. I pray to say thank-you and I pray to ask for forgiveness. I pray to see more clearly and to find the truth. I pray for the people I love and I pray for courage.

FEELING POWERLESS

"We begin to age when, for the very first time, we feel a sense of powerlessness that neutralizes all idea of challenge."

— FRANÇOIS GARAGNON

*A*ging is a physical phenomenon, of course, but it is also a mental phenomenon. We are old when we feel old. At times, we encounter individuals who are physically young, but who are old on the emotional level. At times, we meet elderly people who are very young at heart. When we are aware of the relationship between our bodies and our minds, we can see that people who are mentally old undoubtedly accelerate the process of physical aging. And people who are mentally young undoubtedly slow down their physical aging. The solution lies in our ability to cultivate attitudes and behaviours that encourage vitality, optimism and action.

Today, I know that my mental age and my physical age are two different things. I can stay young by cultivating positive mental attitudes.

HEALTH AND WELL-BEING

*W*e are increasingly aware that health and well-being are directly related to emotions and attitudes. Some people even claim that most physiological illnesses and discomforts are psychosomatic, that there is a close link between our state of mind and our physical health. We know that we are responsible for our own health and when we fall into the trap of illness, life becomes a horrendous chore.

Today, I work to maintain and strengthen my health. By eating properly, by getting enough sleep and rest, by staying fit, I can ward off illness. A caring, loving and vigilant attitude toward myself paves the way to health and well-being.

A WORLD OF SUFFERING

"Although the world is full of suffering, it is also full of the overcoming of it."
— HELEN KELLER

I nitially, most people claim that they are happy or fairly happy. But when you look beyond the surface, you see that these same people want to change certain important aspects of their lives. Deep down, they feel that something is missing and that something is a source of dissatisfaction, perhaps even of suffering. Tucked away in some part of their lives, doubts and problems make their lives much less happy. Unknowingly, such individuals often spend an entire lifetime trying to solve their problems and the hidden suffering. Think simply of the person who is unable to build lasting relationships, the person who constantly experiences health problems or the person who never manages to surmount financial problems.

Today, I understand that we all have problems and we all have sources of suffering in our lives. I know that eventually, I will be capable of identifying and eliminating the main source of my problems.

TIME

"Children begin by loving their parents; as they grow older they judge them; sometimes they forgive them."

— OSCAR WILDE

*W*e say that time heals all wounds. We also see that our relationships change over time. A human relationship is not static. Rather, it is a form of dynamic interaction that changes and is transformed with time and the experiences life brings. A relationship can go through difficult times and easy times. We must determine whether a relationship is fundamentally good and if it is, we must choose to weather the phases it goes through as the years go by.

Today, I know that human relationships are changed and transformed as the years go by. Over time, if they are fundamentally sound, we can resolve most of the difficulties we encounter in our relationships.

INSPIRATION

"I learned from them that inspiration does not come like a bolt, nor is it kinetic, energetic striving, but it comes into us slowly and quietly and all the time, though we must regularly and every day give it a little chance to start flowing, prime it with a little solitude and idleness."
— BRENDA UELAND

*W*hen we set out to solve a problem or carry out a plan, we must build a framework that encourages inspiration and creativity. To some extent, we are artists looking for our next source of inspiration to complete a work of art. We are not motivated by stress, pressure or obligations, but by the desire to create something good, something beautiful and something lasting.

Today, I know that I will find the inspiration I need.

THE BENEFITS OF SLEEP

"I was looking for an answer to a scientific problem. I had spent months examining the issue to find the answer to an enigma that was bothering me. Each day, I mulled over the problem. On one particularly disruptive night, the solution came to me in a dream. I awoke immediately, wrote down the solution on a piece of paper and went back to sleep. The next day, when I looked closely at what I had written, I realized that I had solved my problem in a dream."

— JOHN CHARLES S.

*W*hen we seek to solve a problem, a good night's sleep can be very useful in helping us to see things more clearly. Often, when we are tired, a problem can seem insurmountable. But with a bit of rest and the peace that sleep brings, we can tackle a problem more clearly and with a stronger sense of objectivity and detachment.

Today, I know that sleep can be very beneficial.

PATIENCE

"Patience is the courage of virtue."
— BERNARDIN DE SAINT-PIERRE

*I*n a fast-paced era, it may seem old-fashioned to speak of patience. And yet some things will always require time. Reaching our objectives requires time. Planning a project and carrying it out requires several steps. I must be patient and I must be careful not to overlook the important steps that ensure my success. At times, I can be in a hurry to reach my goal and I can make costly mistakes that jeopardize my entire project.

Today, I see how important patience is to my success. I cannot wait patiently. I must take action each day. However, I will take the time and make the effort required to reach my objectives.

RENEWAL

"As long as there is life, there is hope."
— JOHN LENNON

*E*ach moment brings new possibilities, new windows we can look through. Like the cells in our bodies, at every moment, we can undergo renewal. Each day is an opportunity for renewal. We can look at a situation from a new perspective, in a new light. We can take advantage of each moment and we can see that we live in a constant state of change and renewal.

Today, I see that my happiness and my success are based on my ability to adapt and to change. I do not dwell on any one incident in my life. Each day is an opportunity for renewal and in each moment, I see a new possibility; with each breath, I feel a new sense of hope.

LENDING A HELPING HAND

"As long as you keep a person down, some part of you has to be down there to hold him down, so it means you cannot soar as you otherwise might."

— MARION ANDERSON

*W*hen we do a favour for someone or help someone out, we contribute to elevating our inner being and we rise above the simple fight for survival. Similarly, when we refuse to lend a helping hand to those around us, we shift the focus to our own difficulties.

Today, I realize that I cannot grow in isolation. I cannot elevate my inner being if I turn my back on those who are suffering. I must build close and caring relationships with those who share my life.

TRUE LOVE

"True love is a gift we cannot achieve through effort. It is a gift of the soul, not the consequence of a conscious process. It is not an objective we can target, but a treasure that is given to us freely. So when love seems to appear spontaneously, make no special effort, let it envelop you! When your intimate relationships offer you moments that are both grandiose and unexpected, do not seek to analyze or repeat them; open your heart and let it soar into the light."

— DAPHNE ROSE KINGMA

ove is not something you can find on demand. A person can do many different things to achieve it, but love can remain illusive. Books that claim to provide the magic recipe to teach us how to find love and how to keep it, how to find a life partner, very often fail to point out that there is nothing we can do to win someone's love. Love is given freely or not at all. We cannot force someone to love us. And often, despite all of our efforts, we cannot prevent someone from loving us. We love spontaneously and our actions can encourage or destroy love. The choice is ours.

Today, I understand that love is not something I can demand.

THE POWER OF TRUTH

"... as long as there is a distinction between what should be and what is, conflicts will arise systematically, and all source of conflict is a waste of energy."

— KRISHNAMURTI

There is one true value in this universe: the power of truth. Truth constantly seeks to manifest itself because in and of itself, it is the highest manifestation of our awareness and our spirituality. But here on earth, truth can be very rare. We must be very determined and vigilant to see the truth in certain things and certain events. It is as if this universe we share has been founded on an enormous lie and through its courage, its work and its intelligence, our soul must find the path to truth.

Today, I seek the path that will lead me to truth.

CONTENTMENT

"The world is full of people looking for spectacular happiness while they snub contentment."
— DOUG LARSON

I n our endless search for happiness, we have forgotten that it may well be that total happiness does not exist in its purest form. And even if we reach a very high level of joy and happiness, the hardships and difficulties of day-to-day life can rob us of our achievement. However, it is completely normal and positive to seek happiness. On our road to happiness, we can enjoy the rewards of work well done, the joy of stimulating encounters and the satisfaction of dedication and commitment. This awareness is not perfect happiness, but rather the varying degree of contentment and satisfaction we experience in our lives.

Today, even though I am not totally happy, I can see that my life is filled with many sources of joy and satisfaction.

THE POWER OF LOVE

"When we love someone, we allow them to have an impact on us, we allow them to touch us, to urge us on in one direction or another. We wear different clothes and adopt new hair styles. We travel. We give up bad habits. We do things we were afraid of doing until now. And we do all these things not because the other person asks or demands that we do them, but because through their very presence, their example, we feel inclined to change. In fact, we often change without even realizing it."

— DAPHNE ROSE KINGMA

A love relationship is a dynamic framework for growth and change. Two people in a relationship have a natural ability to adapt. We are not forced to change or to compromise. To build a solid relationship, we make the choices that create harmony. Big or small, the choices we make each day can reinforce the ties that keep us together.

Today, I know that a relationship is a dynamic framework for change. And I know that I have the ability to love and to adapt.

PRECONCEIVED IDEAS

*O*ur preconceived ideas are true barriers to our development. We must develop the ability to identify such barriers and to overcome them. We think that these barriers are external, but in reality they are part of our perceptions and they limit our potential to achieve success. Some preconceived ideas are focused on our own abilities. These barriers are the most challenging because they limit our ability to act and to succeed. Throughout our lives, we must examine our ideas, attitudes and perceptions so that they do not hinder our progress. Only when we are capable of identifying our personal barriers clearly can we set out on the road to success and happiness.

Today, I examine the preconceived ideas that hinder my personal development.

OVERCOMING OUR LIMITATIONS

"For some people, hardships are a pretext for discouragement. For others, they are a reason to reach beyond personal limitation."
— FRANÇOIS GARAGNON

L ife is a series of challenges and barriers. Our attitude to such barriers — not the barriers themselves — determines the quality of our lives. If we want to succeed, if we want to be happy, we must surmount life's barriers and take on its challenges. For example, we may be burdened with financial problems. This is a barrier we can and should overcome. This barrier is both external and internal. Financial difficulties take shape in the material world and inside ourselves, in the form of limitations. Barriers are not walls or prisons, they are obstacles on the path to happiness and we alone decide whether we will overcome them.

Today, I know that I can handle all of the challenges and overcome all of the barriers that I may encounter on my path to success and happiness.

CONFESSION

"For him who confesses, shams are over and realities have begun; he has exteriorized his rottenness. If he has not actually gotten rid of it, he at least no longer smears it over with a hypocritical show of virtue."

— WILLIAM JAMES

*W*hen we make a mistake or when we hurt someone, we know that we have. We carry the burden of the harm we cause and it hinders our progress and stunts our growth. Organized religions have found mechanisms — such as confession, in the case of Christians — to help people break free from their own transgressions and the guilt and remorse they create in the hearts of those responsible for them. Regardless of whether or not we are believers, we must find an alternative way to right our wrongs and to shoulder our responsibility for them.

Today, I can face the music. I admit my wrongs and I take responsibility for them.

LISTENING TO OURSELVES

"If you do not express your own original ideas, if you do not listen to your own being, you will have betrayed yourself."

— ROLLO MAY

*E*ach person has something to bring to this world. Each person has the responsibility of finding self-fulfillment and achieving his or her ideas and dreams. When we express our potential and when we make our dreams come true, we are faithful and loyal to our inner selves.

Today, I see that I am here to find total fulfillment.

THE PRESENT

"Do not hold on too strongly to what has been. Do not hold on too strongly to what could be. Memories and hopes are not the present reality. Instead, hold on to what is."

— FRANÇOIS GARAGNON

*M*emories belong to the past. Hopes concerning the future are part of the reality that we can anticipate or that we want to anticipate. Memories and hopes have their own reality. They exist within us. They are part of our secret garden. Memories and hopes have no material form in the present. The present consists of what is happening around me and within me at this moment. It is the source of experience. Experience is living and creative since it puts me into direct contact with the here and now.

Today, I am open and receptive to the present.

THE PATH WE TAKE

"A relationship is a process, not a destination. It is a sacred interpersonal environment for the growth of two souls; it is the experience of the growth in your individual awareness, in the presence of another human being whose awareness is also undergoing a growth process."
— DAPHNE ROSE KINGMA

A relationship never stands still. A relationship is a dynamic undertaking that calls for the active participation of two individuals. A relationship can change when two people love each other, respect each other and are able to communicate and set common goals. The partners in a relationship agree to travel on the same road toward their common objectives. And along the way, they agree to support one another. When we view marriage or a relationship as an end in itself, we are poorly prepared to face the problems and the barriers we all encounter sooner or later. When we view our relationship as a process, we accept the fact that change is part of it.

Today, I see my relationship as a dynamic process, focused on self-discovery.

OUR DESTINY

"We must learn to embrace our destiny. That infinitesimal moment in time when nothing can become something."
— FRANÇOIS GARAGNON

*M*any people entertain the false notion that to get something, we have to use something else as its basis; for example, if I want my own business, I need start-up capital; to be happy in a relationship, I need the right partner; to succeed financially, I need a good job. In other words if I want to have, I have to have to begin with.

However, we can see things differently. We can do and be, and having will come naturally. For example, I can decide that I am an artist and then I can do everything that an artist must do. Eventually, what an artist usually has will come to me. Or I can say that I am an entrepreneur and then I can do what an entrepreneur does — the having part will follow.

Today, I know that having does not generate having. Before I can have, I must do and be.

POETRY

"Poets are ordinary people, they live just around the corner and they do ordinary things: they do the laundry and they stir the soup."
— NAOMI SHIHAB NYE

There is an inherent poetry in life itself. The poet is able to see and feel life's inherent poetry. He sees the magic in movement and discovers the secrets tucked away, inside the things we see every day. The poet sees life's poetry and seeks to transform the most ordinary of things into poetic instruments.

Today, I discover the poet in myself. I can look at life with the eyes of a poet, I can change my life by filling it with colour, movement and music.

GOING WITH THE FLOW

"We flow naturally and we are malleable. But painful experiences, failures and negative attitudes can make us increasingly rigid. We must seek to break free from the burden we carry within us, making us very material beings."

— ANONYMOUS

W e hear people say that as we grow older, we become less flexible, more set in our ways. We can all decide to become more flexible as we grow older. Life demands a great deal of flexibility. We can adapt by acquiring new perceptions and new behaviours. And we can go with the flow without the need to make fundamental compromises. By agreeing to look at life from different standpoints, by agreeing to take on another person's perceptions, we can see things more clearly. It is impossible to be happy when we are inflexible and intransigent. When we are rigid and closed, we succeed only in isolating ourselves.

Today, I seek my fundamental nature. Flexibility is a natural part of my being.

SEEING

"When I was young, adults used to tell me: You'll see, just wait until you're 50. I am 50 now, and I haven't seen anything."

— ERIK SATIE

*W*e can wonder about the deep meaning of life. We can wonder why we are here, on this tiny planet moving through space. We can wrack our brains trying to find the real meaning of life and the true sense of the gestures we make. Or we can live each day to the fullest by doing the best we can.

Today, I know that I must live each day to the fullest.

THE LAST WORD

"Some people always want the last word. I leave it to them."

— FRANCINE BOIVIN

*L*ife is too short for fighting. Of course, conflicts and misunderstandings can arise. But some individuals spend their entire lives fighting against one thing or another. Maybe they have something to prove.

Today, I see that disputes and conflicts lead nowhere. I am not here to do battle, but to learn and create. I leave the last word to the people who seem to want it.

REAPING WHAT WE SOW

"If you respect others, they will respect you. Similarly, if you show them no respect..."
— ALBERT LAROCHE

We all know people who do a lot of harm by being discourteous and disrespectful in their dealings with others. When we are polite and respectful, we attract respect. When we are impolite and impatient with the people we interact with, we attract conflict and bitterness. Respect and courtesy contribute to positive human relations.

Today, I know that to be respected, I must act respectfully and courteously in all situations and under all circumstances.

TAKING TIME TO REST

"Just for today, I won't make a list of things to do!"

— GABRIELLE COURCHESNE

In our endless quest for material success and financial security, we sometimes forget to relax and take time out to rest. There are many ways to relax: watching a movie; going for a long walk; playing games with our children; taking a long, hot bath; reading a good book. We all need to take the time to rest and have fun.

Today, I take the time I need to relax and have fun. I like my work and I accept my responsibilities, but I can pamper myself from time to time.

THE GREATEST REWARD

"Make a point of telling people how good you feel when they do a job correctly and how much it helps the organization and their colleagues."
— KENNETH BLANCHARD AND SPENCER JOHNSON

*A*n employee's greatest reward isn't his salary, his fringe benefits or the prestige attached to his job within the organization. The greatest reward is the appreciation of colleagues and superiors. Too often, we forget an important point: stating out loud and sincerely how deeply we appreciate those who work with us and share our lives.

Today, I take the time to compliment, to appreciate and to encourage those who share my life.

WHAT SCHOOL DOESN'T TEACH YOU

*E*ducation is certainly a precious asset that contributes much to our success. However, many lessons are learned not in school, but in everyday life. In life, we are confronted with very real demands. We must learn to work as part of a team and to respect the wishes and expectations of others. To be happy, it is crucial that we learn from the lessons life brings us.

Each day is an opportunity to learn a new lesson. When we are open to life's lessons, we bring optimism and enthusiasm to our experiences. Life teaches us new ways to act and new ways to see things. When we are open to these lessons, we fulfill a fundamental mission.

Today, I am open to life's lessons.

A SHORT PRAYER

*T*oday, I ask God to guide my thoughts and my actions. Today, I agree to place my life in His hands, to relinquish my life to His will and His goodness. Today, I seek to be an instrument of God and I seek to spread goodness and kindness to all those who cross my path. Today, I give up the fight to be right and to win at all costs and I relinquish my fate to God, to His greatness and to His love for every living being.

Today, I ask God to guide my thoughts and my actions.

THE PEOPLE I KNOW

"You may be older, you may have gained weight, your hair may be gray, but for your friends, you're still the person they met at school."
— MARIAN GARRETTY

The people who know us best see us differently from those who have just met us for the first time. Of course, we have a real, flesh-and-blood person standing before us. But when we know and like them, physical appearance is much less important. When we get to know someone well, we can establish a true relationship with them. We do not build a relationship with a body. We build a relationship with human beings. After a while, we hardly see the body, so strong is our relationship with the being. Sensuality, tenderness, warmth, authentic beauty are all things that emanate from the being, not the body.

Today, I know that my relationships are with other beings, not other bodies.

FRIENDS

"A friend is someone who knows everything there is to know about you and loves you anyway."
— CHRISTI-MARY WARNER

A true friend plays on the same team as we do. He is prejudiced in our favour. And despite all of the things we may have said or done during our lifetime, a true friend will always understand our point of view and our motivations.

There is a special kind of synergy in a friendship. Friendship is a co-creation, a type of practical symbiosis. As a friendship develops, we become a little more like our friend and our friend becomes a little more like us. The communication between true friends is always good because friends have the same viewpoints and the same realities.

Today, I take pleasure in the fact that I have built solid and lasting friendships over the years.

I CAN FIND THE LOVE I SEEK

*T*oday, regardless of where I may be or who I am with, I will recognize the love I seek. I am a luminous being and I am fundamentally good, therefore I have nothing to fear. I can share. I can listen. I can use every opportunity to let my true colours shine through.

Today, I am at the right place, at the right time.

WALKING IN ANOTHER PERSON'S SHOES

"Tolerance is the charity of intelligence."
— JULES LEMAÎTRE

*L*etting another person be himself, have his own ideas, habits and beliefs and respecting his tastes is allowing him to live and think freely and differently. Tolerance begins at the heart of our society: the family. Parents look on lovingly as their children take their first steps; they patiently share their wisdom and experience; they encourage and foster perseverance. The child needs time to learn and to understand; knowledge and wisdom are acquired gradually. What we say and how we say it stays in our children's memories. It is not uncommon to see hatred transmitted from one generation to the next.

Today, I see that I can be tolerant; I want to work with others and I want to live in harmony. Team work is often crucial to success; therefore I am open to ideas, to personalities and to the way others choose to live.

SURVIVING

"The turning point in the process of growing up is when you discover the core of strength within you that survives all hurt."

— MAX LERNER

*W*e all go through major difficulties. We all have failed and we all have experienced significant losses. What makes us different is the fact that we are still here, with open eyes and an open heart. We have chosen to continue growing and to continue creating in spite of our difficulties. Within ourselves, we have found the source of wisdom and power that lets us love and continue to grow.

Today, I am in contact with the inner source of wisdom and power that pushes me ever forward.

HIDING OUR IMPERFECTIONS

"He who conceals his disease cannot expect to be cured."

— ETHIOPIAN PROVERB

*T*he world is full of imperfections, just as it is filled with beauty. We can see a thing of beauty and be distracted by its imperfections or we can accept its imperfections and enjoy its beauty. In relationships, we accept our partners' imperfections because we want to be with them and we know that imperfections are insignificant. Rather than hiding or concealing them, we should show imperfections. When we expose our imperfections, we can live and breathe freely and we can be ourselves. When I am myself, my true beauty surfaces.

Today, I no longer hide my imperfections. I am who I am.

BEING OPEN

"Nothing can make your happier and nothing can make you feel more like your true self than a genuine and honest emotional relationship with another human being. Nothing is more wonderful than being able to tell someone who you are, to open your heart, to show your true colours, to meet another person on the same level."
— DAPHNE ROSE KINGMA

A relationship or a friendship should make us feel safe. I feel safe when I know that I can truly count on the other person. A safe relationship is one that shows me that the other person's commitment is strong enough to withstand life's trials and tribulations. In a safe relationship, I can be myself and I can communicate freely. The opportunity to be honest at all times means that I can always be myself.

Today, I seek to make each of my major relationships and friendships havens that make me feel safe.

THE DREAMS OF OUR YOUTH

"In our childhood, there always comes a time when a door opens to let our future come in."
— GRAHAM GREENE

W hen we are young, we imagine all sorts of things about our adult life. We peer into the future and we plan the career we will have, the life we will have. We idealize the future and we see it as a time filled with success, love and stability. However, reality teaches us that adult life can be tumultuous. We must work hard to achieve our objectives. Often, when we achieve what we thought we wanted, we discover that what we so coveted fails to live up to our expectations or our deepest wishes. Life puts many obstacles in our way and soon, we see that the dreams of our youth were just that: the dreams of the young.

However, there is something very authentic in the dreams of our youth and they tell us who we truly are. It is for each of us to decide whether we have been loyal to our true selves.

Today, I look at my life and I see that I have been loyal to my true self. I have had to compromise along the way, but fundamentally, I have been loyal to my ideals and to my dreams.

BEING TRUE

"Strength is expressed in our ability to be brutally honest with ourselves. Only when we have the courage to face things as they are, without illusion or deceit, can a light be shed on the event to guide us to the right path."

— THE I CHING

When we refer to honesty, we think of the quality of not robbing or cheating others. However, honesty was first associated with the concept of honour. Someone honest was someone fair, worthy of respect and esteem.

Honesty is a crucial quality. First, we must be fiercely honest with ourselves. We must look at things as they truly are and we must be capable of relying on ourselves. We must be capable of knowing that we have done all that we could do to keep our word. We must be capable of coping with difficult situations and problems unreservedly, knowing that we can find the best solution. Moreover, when we are honest and sincere with others, we earn their respect and trust. When we are honest, we create a climate of emotional stability and security and we can build solid relationships.

Today, I see honesty as essential to my personal development and my inner peace.

SAYING THANK YOU

"If the only prayer you say in your whole life is 'thank you', that would suffice."
— MEISTER ECKHART

Today, I know that I can fuel my dissatisfaction but instead, I choose to say thank you. I look around and I see that I am blessed. I am alive and I have the gift of awareness. I can make my own choices and I can grow each and every day. Today, I am filled with gratitude; my life is full and I am free to live it to the fullest.

POSITIVE THINKING

"If you think you can, you can. And if you think you can't, you can't."

— MARY KAY ASH

No one can question the value and power of positive thinking. Those who think positively tend to be happier, to be more successful on the professional and material levels and to enjoy more satisfying relationships. So why wait? Why not adopt positive mental attitudes right now?

Today, I adopt a positive mental attitude. Armed with this attitude, I know that I can overcome all obstacles and I can grow and live each day with joy and a sense of satisfaction.

THE WHISPERS OF ANGELS

"If you are seeking creative ideas, go out walking. Angels whisper to a man who goes for a walk."

— RAYMOND IMMON

*I*n the past few years, angels have become very popular. Many books have been written on the subject, explaining how we can contact our angels, how to recognize our guardian angels and how angels can protect us, guide us and save us. Without entering the debate on whether or not angles truly exist and whether or not they have curative powers, we should consider one fact: angels are not part of our tangible human relationships. Unfortunately (or perhaps fortunately), we do not live in the immaterial world, but in the material world shared by all human beings. Nothing can replace concrete actions and their repercussions on concrete reality.

Today, I see how important it is to invest my energy in concrete human relationships and exchanges.

I AM FANTASTIC!

*T*oday, I know that I am a fantastic human being who deserves to be loved and to find self-fulfillment. I have broken down the inner barriers that prevented me from being myself and from shining like a divine light. I am a child of God, I have my place in the universe and I seek to grow each and every day.

Today, I am a child of God and I know that I have my very own place in the universe.

STRENGTH AND WEAKNESS

*"By chance, man can reign over the entire earth
for a given time; but by virtue of love and goodness, he can reign over the world forever."*
— LAO-TZU

Many people still do not understand that we cannot dominate, control or enslave others using force and aggression. Our societies are increasingly violent and we try to settle our differences using intimidation and violence. Violence breeds force. Force provokes an equally strong reaction. Such are the laws of the universe. Luckily, only goodness, kindness and compassion can break down the walls that separate us.

**Today, I see that goodness is the path that
leads to higher levels of awareness and action.
I refuse to use intimidation and aggression and
I adopt attitudes and behaviours founded on
love and compassion.**

THE RIGHT TO BE DIFFERENT

"Freedom means the right to be different, the right to be oneself."

— IRA EINSENSTEIN

We often see teenagers exercising their right to be different. They seek to build a world that belongs to them and that resembles them more than it resembles their parents. Often, teenagers want to make themselves different from some standpoint or from other individuals of their own age. However, adult life encourages us to conform. On several levels, to succeed socially and professionally, we are forced to play the game according to a specific set of rules. This process of adaptation and conformity is undoubtedly valuable, but it should not force us to give up our individuality.

All individuals have their own reality and special characteristics that make each of us unique. By expressing our differences, we express our individual beauty. There is no need to shock or to go to absurd lengths to be different. Each of us is already different. All we need do is express our differences while acknowledging the realities of others.

Today, I understand that I must adapt to the demands of my environment, but I can also express my individuality.

FEAR

"Fears are educated into us, and can, if we wish, be educated out."
— KARL A. MENNINGER

*I*n one way or another, our parents, our teachers and the media cultivate fear and distrust. We learn very young that the world can be a threatening and dangerous place. We know that our parents and teachers love us and seek to protect us, but the media seeks to exploit and reinforce our fears. We must learn to judge the world fairly.

We may be called upon to go out into the world to build an interesting and satisfying life around our relationships with other human beings. To do so, we must agree to take risks. To succeed and to find what we seek in life, we must confront and overcome our fears.

Today, I know that life involves a certain number of risks. I will be vigilant, but I resolve to confront my fears.

DETERMINATION

"Let me tell you the secret that made it possible for me to achieve my goal. My strength lies solely in my determination."

— LOUIS PASTEUR

Today, I know that I am determined. When I look at my life and when I see all the difficulties that I have overcome, I realize that I am determined. Sooner or later, my determination will make it possible for me to reach my goals.

OPENING OUR EYES

"If I were to begin life again, I should want it as it was. I would only open my eyes a little more."
— JULES RENARD

*W*e sometimes forget simply to look at the world around us, to truly see it. A wonderful world of individuals and things awaits only our discovery. We can take the time to see and to appreciate the beauty around us.

Today, I see that life is filled with beauty and adventure and I open my eyes to better see and admire it.

NOTHING CAN PREVENT ME FROM GROWING

"We always find what we seek. The answer is always there and, if we take the time, it will be revealed to us."

— THOMAS MERTON

*W*e are among those who have made the conscious choice to grow. We want to surpass our initial limitations and materialize our dream of being all that we can truly be. We seek our true essence and life's experiences inevitably guide us through a process of gradual discovery. We know that there is no goal more noble or more spiritual than the emancipation of our true self.

Today, I know that nothing can prevent me from growing. I am among those who have chosen to live in awareness and enlightenment.

WE ARE UNIQUE

"Beauty is something rare and wonderful that the artist, in the depths of a tormented soul, extracts from universal chaos. And when beauty is created, not everyone can see it."
— SOMERSET MAUGHAM

*W*e are unique in the sense that not everyone is aware and capable of living and acting completely consciously. We are unique because we are incapable of turning a blind eye. We truly see the world around us, its beauty and its challenges. With this awareness, this vision and this discernment come a certain number of duties and responsibilities. Our first and foremost duty is to grow.

Today, I know that I am a person who lives with my eyes wide open on the world. I could never deny this reality. I accept the prime responsibility of awareness: to grow.

GOOD AND EVIL

"It is not living according to science that brings happiness, nor even uniting all sciences into one group; happiness is the knowledge of the sole science of good and evil."

— PLATO

*W*hat makes us different from criminals and cowards is the fact that we know the difference between good and evil. Society can arm itself with legions of police forces, surveillance cameras and an infinite number of prisons; the effort will be pointless. Individuals must know how to behave decently. They must know the difference between good and evil and they must be capable of choosing good over evil. When individuals are not capable of resisting evil, society must intervene to protect others. But first and foremost, each of us has the responsibility of exercising self-control.

Today, I know the difference between good and evil and I choose to do good.

ENDING OUR SUFFERING

"Suffering is a journey which has an end."
— MATTHEW FOX

I t is completely normal to feel a sense of suffering after a failure, a loss or a problem. But life is so much more than suffering. Suffering eventually comes to an end. Unfortunately, many people think that life is synonymous with suffering. They go from one loss or one failure to another to confirm and reinforce their desire to suffer. They have the false impression that suffering gives meaning to their lives.

Today, I see that suffering must come to an end. Life is more than suffering. It is also joy, inner peace and happiness.

TODAY, I LISTEN TO MY HEART

*T*oday, I listen to my heart because I know that it cannot lie. For a long time I thought that I could find intellectual answers to my existential questions. But as time went by, I realized that I could not live solely in my head.

Today, I know that my heart can give me the answers I need.

THE SOURCE OF SUCCESS

"Do not dwell on your failures. It may well be that in them, you will find the resources you need to succeed."

— FRANÇOIS GARAGNON

O bviously, no one seeks to fail. However, failures are part of life. We can run from failures by being conservative and by avoiding all type of questionable action or we can take action while accepting that failures are part of the growth and learning process.

Today, I take action because I know that I must take action. I know that I may fail at times and I will use my failures to learn and to grow.

OUR DESTINY

I n the '60s, we were convinced that we could change the world. The entire planet seemed to be in a state of effervescence. We talked about brotherly love, cooperation and putting an end to the establishment. However, as the years went by the dream of changing the world faded, giving way to a more moderate vision of things and the practical considerations of everyday life. The world still needs improving, but we see no social movement looking to bring us in this direction.

Today, I see that there are many things we can do to build a better world. I want to do my share to reach that goal.

BEING TOLD THAT WE ARE VALUABLE

"We hear so much praise for modesty and self-effacement that we are uncomfortable when the time comes to hear that we have a personal value."

— SUE PATTON THOELE

Today, I know that despite my mistakes, despite my imperfections and despite the progress I have yet to make, I am an extremely valuable person. Deep inside, I know who I am. I am a loving and generous person who wants to do my best. I have many wonderful qualities that I let shine through each and every day. My loved one can easily see that I am loving and altruistic.

I DESERVE TO BE HAPPY

*T*oday, I deserve to be happy. I feel that the universe as a whole is open to me and that I can touch the stars. When I look around me, I see that life is exciting and I feel that I have my place in this wonderful world.

Today, I am a child of the stars and I shine with joy and love.

STUBBORNNESS

"There is no greater weakness than stubbornness. If you cannot yield, if you cannot learn that there must be compromises in life — you lose."
— MAXWELL MALTZ

*P*rofessional poker players know that to win, you have to know when to stand firm and when to step down. The idea is to make gains while minimizing losses, surviving until the next time. This analogy applies to life. To play life's game, we have to take risks while minimizing the potential losses, without exhausting our resources. We should never try to win every match. Rather, we should focus on the game as a whole, understanding where our interests lie over the long term. We can even go so far as to accept a short-term loss to obtain a long-term victory.

Today, in all situations I choose judicious analysis over stubbornness. I have no need to win in all situations. Instead, I focus on winning in the long term.

THE RHYTHM OF LOVE

"These days, with our heavy and complicated schedules, we can lose contact with the people we love, sometimes for days and days. This is precisely why we need to make an effort to control our obligations and our plans, but also the rhythm that is crucial to any close relationship."
— DAPHNE ROSE KINGMA

*E*ach relationship has its needs and its expectations. Like a flower garden, a relationship requires that we be present and that we be caring. Modern society requires that we go away from home often and it pushes us to build a career. To succeed on the material level, we often have to work long hours, relegating our intimate and social relationships to the background. We run the risk of slowly losing sight of the vital needs inherent in our close relationships. We should know that financial success has no value if we cannot share it with those we love. Building healthy and lasting relationships takes time and energy. We should have enough respect for those we love to adapt to each relationship's needs and rhythms.

Today, I see that my relationships are the most precious assets in my life and so I will take the time I need to nurture them.

LOOKING AT WHERE WE ARE TODAY

"Don't let life discourage you; everyone who got where he is had to begin where he was."
— R.L. EVANS

*A*t times we can feel discouraged when we see that despite our efforts and our good intentions, we still have not managed to travel the road that leads to self-satisfaction. But even the longest journey begins with a single step. Instead of focusing on how much ground we have left to cover, we should concentrate on the knowledge that we are growing closer and closer to our ultimate objective, no matter what.

Today, I can travel the road to happiness and serenity. Despite the obstacles and difficulties I may encounter, I am proud that I can continue moving forward.

OUR ONLY TRUE ADVISOR

"He that, to what he sees, adds observation, and to what he reads, reflection, is on the right road to knowledge."

— CALEB COLTON

R eading self-help books, attending conferences given by famous gurus and listening to the advice of enlightened individuals is not enough; we must learn to think for ourselves. Ultimately, we must discover what makes us happy, where our truth lies and what we can accept.

Today, I understand that I am my best and my only true advisor. The people who are close to me can give me their suggestions, comments and advice, but in the end, I am the person who is ultimately responsible for my happiness.

INTROSPECTION IS DANGEROUS

"When a person drowns himself in negative thinking he is committing an unspeakable crime against himself."
— MAXWELL MALTZ

Introspection can be dangerous. When we ruminate on dark ideas and withdraw into ourselves to think about one thing or another, we move away from reality. We must try to live not in our own minds, but among the living.

Today, I refuse to entertain negative thoughts. Instead of ruminating on the past, I look outside myself.

BEING RIGHT OR WRONG

*M*ost conflicts result from the fact that we believe we are right and the other person is wrong, and vice versa. Each person stands firm and refuses to yield. Human relations require a much more flexible and conscious approach. No one likes to be told or to admit that he is wrong. It is a matter of personal pride. No one likes to be subjected to domination or criticism. When we are faced with a situation of conflict, in addition to expressing our own opinion, we must seek to understand the other person's point of view. We must ensure that the contact remains polite and cordial. When we stay objective, most conflicts can be resolved.

Today, I see that most conflicts can be resolved as long as I remain flexible and courteous.

REST

*W*e sometimes forget that rest is crucial to our happiness and personal well-being. We can sometimes try so hard and so relentlessly to get a job done that we become unpleasant, vengeful and bad-tempered. When we are involved in a love relationship, when we have family and personal responsibilities, we can forget to get enough rest. When we are tired, we can easily get involved in arguments. We have a hard time finding solutions to everyday problems and we often give in to anger. Rest is beneficial — when we are refreshed and energized, we can face life's demands more confidently.

Today, I am aware that rest is crucial if I want to be happy and in harmony with the people who share my life.

SIMPLE PLEASURES

"One ought, each day at least, to hear a little song, read a good poem, see a fine picture and, if possible, speak a few reasonable words."

— GOETHE

The most satisfying things are sometimes the simplest: a sunny day, birds singing in a garden, a delicious meal, a phone call from an old friend, comfortable slippers, the smell of fresh bread baking in the kitchen, a good movie, a bit of money in the bank. These are simple pleasures that fill our hearts and that remind us that the human experience is beautiful and enjoyable.

Today, I seek simple pleasures because they fill me with joy and peace.

HATRED

"A flower dies, even if we love it. A seed grows, even if we don't love it."

— DOGEN

We can see how some people develop hatred and bitterness. They send out negative feelings, but in the final analysis, by clinging to negative emotions they are most harmful to themselves. Hatred can only sap our energy and hinder our ability to live life to the fullest. Some studies even claim that negative emotions can have an effect on our health. People who hate can be harmful to us. They may start false rumours and make a point of making others miserable. Since we are all on the path we have chosen in life and since we do not want to fight hatred with hatred, we should continue to move forward, with no feeling of intimidation.

Today, I know that I do not need to be loved by everyone to grow. I am here to grow and I will continue to grow despite the obstacles in my path.

ESCAPING THE PAST

*D*ay-to-day life is filled with examples of people who feel resentful of an acquaintance, a colleague, a family member. The resentment may last for days, months or even years. Many of us know people who tearfully recount that a particular person passed away before they were unable to offer forgiveness. This type of story is upsetting and it shows the destructive power of bitterness.

Several religious celebrations offer the faithful the opportunity to forgive those who have offended them: the pilgrimage to Saint Anne d'Auray in France or Yom Kippur in the Jewish faith. We should always remember that the price of bitterness is much too high. When we maintain and nurture our bitterness and refuse to forgive, we pay the highest possible price.

Today, I understand the value of forgiveness. Since I hope that my offenses will be forgiven, I must learn to forgive those who have offended me. When I forgive, I free myself of the burden of anxiety and bitterness, both of which can only be harmful to my inner peace and serenity.

THE ENERGY THAT LIES WITHIN

"The key to a passionate life is to trust the energy within us and to follow wherever it leads."
— SHAKTI GAWAIN

Today, I listen to the vital force within me, my link to the universe. I know that I am a being of light; I have been given this body for a short while, to accomplish a specific mission on earth.

Today, I listen to all of the subtle messages within me and I let them guide me.

THE YOUTH INDUSTRY

*M*ajor pharmaceutical companies invest huge sums to develop drugs designed to slow down the aging process. Already, wealthy individuals seek out doctors who prescribe growth hormones and other similar products to slow down the aging process, or even reverse it. It is a well-known fact that the baby boomer generation refuses to grow old. They are reluctant to give way to the younger generation and they feel that they are being set aside by society.

It is very easy to predict that the new youth industry will introduce a number of interesting rejuvenating cures — cures that can better control the undesirable effects of aging. Nevertheless, despite all our efforts, we will never be able to prevent aging. We should ask ourselves what price we are prepared to pay, socially and physically, to look a few years younger.

Today, I accept the fact that aging is part of my life here on earth.

THE PRINCIPLE OF NON-ACTION

*I*n his book, the Tao Chi Chin, Lao Tsu describes the virtues of non-action. Non-action is the ability to wait, to observe, to listen and to discover before taking action. Each event is driven by its own dynamics in relation to the laws of the universe. At times, the biggest mistake we can make is to act instead of letting things take their course. Impatient individuals do not take the time to discover; they leap to action and as a result, they disturb the natural order of things. They can teach us an important lesson. Action should be in harmony with the situation and sometimes, it is preferable not to take action and to let events follow their course.

Today, I see that hasty action motivated by impatience can be counterproductive. So I observe, I listen and I wait for the right moment to act.

MAJOR AND MINOR VICTORIES

On the road to happiness and serenity, there are small daily victories and major victories. Each day, we can enjoy our small victories: a day of work well done, better communication with a colleague or a family member, a pleasant day spent in the company of a loved one. We should also take note of our major victories: getting through a difficult time while keeping a sense of humour and inner calm, the birth of a healthy child, a better quality of life as the result of a promotion or a successful business transaction; another wedding anniversary. By focusing our attention on victories instead of defeats, we have a better chance of being happy and fulfilled. Life is filled with all sorts of more or less pleasant events. But if we work towards our personal victories, we see that life can be easier and more exciting. Together, we succeed each and every day. Together, we win major and minor victories.

Today, I concentrate on my many victories: small personal victories and life's major victories as well.

THE HEART'S MOUTH

"The heart of a fool is in his mouth, but the mouth of the wise man is found in his heart."
— BENJAMIN FRANKLIN

*T*he wise person has the ability to listen and to hear. He communicates with others. He sees their level of comprehension, their ability to communicate, to understand and to grasp messages from the outside. Aware and sensitive, he adjusts his communication skills to suit the situation. He ensures that he is on the same wavelength as the person he is speaking to and he communicates effectively. His communication is always honest, he speaks of real things and he is always sensitive to the other person's level of awareness. In this way, he establishes positive links with all those who cross his path.

Today, I listen actively and if needed, I adjust the way in which I communicate with others.

CHOOSING OUR ATTITUDES

"The last of the human freedoms is to choose one's attitudes."

— VICTOR FRANKL

*W*e often feel that our attitudes, our way of seeing things, cannot change. However, a more in-depth analysis shows us that we can choose our attitudes. Often, it may be easier to change our attitude to a particular context instead of trying to change the context itself. For example, it is easier for a prisoner to change his attitude to his incarceration than it is for him to escape his confinement. It is often less hard and upsetting to change our attitude to our relationship than it is to go through a divorce. Similarly, it may be more beneficial to change our attitude to a boss than it would be to find a new job. We can change our attitudes because we establish them ourselves, based on considerations and perceptions that may or may not be valid or useful. An attitude that contributes to our survival and to our happiness is positive. A negative attitude contributes to our unhappiness and hinders our chances of survival. We must reinforce our winning attitudes and change our losing attitudes.

Today, I see that I can change my attitudes. When I realize that my attitudes lead to conflict and suffering, I seek to develop new outlooks.

SIMPLICITY

"All we need to be happy we can find here and now: the answer is a simple heart."
— NIKOS KAZANTZAKIS

*W*ithout denying the importance of past events that may have been painful and tragic, we can see that we are not inevitably chained to the demons of the past. Believing the contrary amounts to saying that we are merely puppets, unable to control our own destiny. When we conduct honest business affairs and when we apply sound values in our lives — such as integrity, respect and loyalty — life becomes much less complicated and much easier. True, life is filled with pitfalls and we sometimes feel crushed by our past failures. But when we are determined and loyal to our principles, we run less risk of sinking into depression and anxiety.

Today, I am open and I seek reconciliation rather than conflict. If I rid my life of contention, vengefulness and animosity, I can keep a light heart and a mind that is open only to the positive.

ENDING UNHAPPY RELATIONSHIPS

*H*uman relations should be based on integrity, communication and mutual interest for both parties. We cannot and do not want to be involved in relationships with people we do not trust or who do not share our values of fairness and integrity. When we realize that someone close to us contributes nothing to our well-being, contributing instead to our decline, we should investigate. We should determine whether our feeling is justified or not. Fortunately, we are usually capable of identifying such people fairly quickly and we can rectify the situation or put an end to the relationship. But at times this type of person can hide and can mask his or her true intentions. And so to limit the harm inflicted on us, we must be aware and vigilant as we interact with others.

We may believe that by ending a negative relationship we may suffer more serious consequences than we would should we decide not to take action. But nothing could be more untrue. In the long term, we will emerge the winner because we will have eliminated a problem and restored order in our lives.

Today, I am aware and vigilant so that I can eliminate negative relationships from my life.

A SPIRITUAL UNDERTAKING

"We seek to determine the meaning of a personal relationship by looking at its deepest origins. While in the past our questions were asked to satisfy our emotions, now they are asked to satisfy our souls. We begin to understand that any personal relationship is also a spiritual undertaking that, beyond the happiness it brings us and the loneliness it prevents us from feeling, opens the path to a garden in which our soul can find fulfillment."

— DAPHNE ROSE KINGMA

*A*ny human relationship is a spiritual undertaking in the sense that it involves the voluntary participation of two free and autonomous souls. We are free to choose the type of life we lead, to choose who we want in our relationships and how long these relationships will last. We are free to make a commitment or refuse to commit ourselves. Because we know that we are free to choose, we also know that our choices shape who we are today and who we will be tomorrow. Those who choose to build committed and long-term relationships will always be privileged because by doing so, they are laying down roots and expressing their true natures.

Today, I know that beyond emotional satisfaction, human relationships offer the opportunity of spiritual growth.

A SECOND CHANCE

"When I was 31, I almost drowned in the Pacific Ocean. As I was floating out to sea on the crest of a huge wave, I came to this major realization: "I still have things to learn and accomplish." Fortunately, perhaps miraculously, I came out of the situation alive. Today, at 40, I see that I did indeed have many things to learn and many things to accomplish. I can thank God for giving me a second chance and believe me, I have never taken this second chance lightly in any way."
— PHILIP S.

*L*ife is fragile. We cannot afford to behave as if we are on earth forever. During our stay, there are things to discover, relationships to build, projects to carry out and objectives to reach. We cannot afford to miss an opportunity as sensational as living on this earth.

Today, I make the very most of the beautiful opportunity of life.

MAKING THINGS HAPPEN

O ne of the biggest challenges in the industrial world consists of making things happen. Of course, there is already a great deal of movement on the planet. But when we want to initiate something new, we often encounter a certain form of resistance. New projects and new ideas are greeted with utter indifference. We feel as if we have sunk into a quagmire. In the final analysis, the most important thing is our intention to carry out a project and the determination we will bring to it.

Today, I will not be discouraged by the resistance I must confront as I carry out my plans and projects.

THE POWER OF INTELLIGENCE

*W*e should never underestimate the power of intelligence. We should also realize that intelligence takes many different forms. When we refer to intelligence, we are not necessarily referring to the intellect or the brain. Rather, we are referring to conscious ability. A person may have a very high intelligence quotient, but he or she may not be able to use it. Intelligence consists in finding viable solutions to everyday problems, bringing organization to your work and your life; it is taking care of yourself and your loved one; it is maximizing your potential and making your life a success.

Today, I use my knowledge and my intelligence to be the person I want to be and to do the things I have promised to do. I use my intelligence to find solutions to the problems I must face and to make my life successful and happy. I use my intelligence to serve my family and my community.

TODAY, I THINK OF MYSELF

"It is within our own pleasure that humans truly live; it is in our recreation that we build our true essence."

— AGNES REPPLIER

*T*oday, I think of myself and my needs. This day is devoted to making myself happy by giving myself a gift or by doing an activity that brings me joy and energy. I should not feel guilty because I am taking care of myself. When I feel happy and fulfilled, I am in a better position to take on my responsibilities and the day-to-day challenges of life.

Today, I give myself the gift of this day.

WHERE AM I GOING?

"Wanting to act is not enough to ensure your personal growth; you must know how to act."
— G. LE BON

*H*uman beings ask several fundamental questions. Where am I? Who am I with? Where am I going? The question of our ultimate destination is important and it serves as the basis of our day-to-day work. Unless we can give at least a partial answer to this question, we are like ships sailing aimlessly on the vast waters of the ocean. To have any meaning, to be effective, action must be directed toward a goal.

When we analyze the question, in all likelihood we discover that each of us has goals for the short, medium and long terms; sometimes they are concrete, sometimes they are abstract. For example, I can take night courses to qualify for a promotion; I can embark on a journey of personal growth to live a happier and more serene life. I may want to set up my own business to achieve financial independence. Setting objectives makes it possible for us to give meaning and a precise direction to our action. We move toward a specific destination. And when we have reached that destination, we will know that our action was not in vain.

Today, my action has a meaning and a direction. Day after day, inevitably, I am closer and closer to my destination.

A WHOLE LIFETIME

"Will you love me in December and in May?
Will you love me in that good old way?
When my hair will be gray,
Will you kiss me and will you say
That you love me in December and in May?"
— JAMES J. WALKER

*M*any people live with the fear that they will be less desirable as the years go by. They are afraid to lose their charms and that they will no longer be capable of attracting the love and the tenderness they so need to feel alive and wanted. They fear the loneliness that comes with old age, abandonment and isolation. These fears do have a basis in reality. All too often we see elderly people who are very alone.

However, we should be hopeful and we should keep in mind that the people who are reaching their retirement age today are much better prepared to take on its challenges. They plan for their senior years and they remain active through a variety of professional and social activities. Most importantly, they have the type of solid experience that is increasingly recognized as valuable.

Today, I see that time is passing and I know that one day, my life will change. I plan to live an active and stimulating life until I take my last breath.

BEING ALONE WITH YOURSELF

"When you create a tolerable world for yourself, you create a tolerable world for others."
— ANAIS NIN

*T*oday, I realize that I need to spend time alone with myself. The time I spend alone — away from distractions, demands and the noise of day-to-day living — lets me make contact with my inner self and lets me find new energy. I like to share my life with others. I like to help and to give my tenderness and support to the people who share my life, but I also like to spend time alone. When I am alone, I feel that I can relax and get in touch with my true feelings.

Today, I take a little time to be with myself, alone.

HARDER DAYS

*S*ome days are harder than others. There are days when nothing seems to go right. There are days when doing the simplest things seems complicated, when we feel that we should have stayed in bed.

On such days, we can take the time to look around and to see that despite everything, life is good. Even the most difficult of times can bring us a form of joy. The joy of being alive, of being capable of facing adversity and triumphing over it.

All in all, I feel satisfied. In difficult times, I can convince myself that tomorrow will be a better day and I know that life's day-to-day hardships serve to remind us that we are alive.

Today, I will do my best and I will get through the day. Today, I will try to keep my sense of humour even if those who share my life seem to have lost theirs.

LIVING LIFE AT YOUR OWN PACE

"If you can just observe who you are and move with it, then you will find that it is possible to go infinitely far."

— J. KRISHNAMURTI

*W*e each have our own pace. Each of us dances to our own rhythm. Some people are very quick, others are very slow. Some can absorb experiences and new lessons rapidly, others need more time to digest each experience and to put new knowledge into practice. Those who live at a quick pace easily lose their patience when they interact with individuals who like to take things slower. And those whose pace is not particularly quick feel rushed and exasperated by the demands of people who want to get things done in an expeditious way. The only conclusion is that each of us must live life at our own specific pace.

Today, I respect my rhythm. I listen to the inner music that transforms my life into a dance with myself and those around me.

ENCOURAGING INSTEAD OF CRITICIZING

"Tolerance, like humour, is a quality that we often demand of others, but that we do not always offer ourselves."

— FRANÇOIS GARAGNON

We can see the effect of criticism in the facial expressions of others. When we criticize them or speak harshly to them, they withdraw and fall silent. We can also see that criticism is not very effective in motivating people to improve their behaviour. Criticism is often the first reaction to something that displeases us. This initial reaction is rarely the right reaction since it is neither constructive nor well thought out.

Today, I rely on encouragement rather than criticism. Instead of reacting spontaneously and resorting to criticism, I take a few minutes to consider the situation. I seek to understand it and I use words of encouragement to motivate others.

WONDERMENT

"If you can keep a sense of wonderment in the face of the day-to-day miracles in your life, your pain will seem no less wonderful than your joy."
— KAHLIL GIBRAN

*W*hen you stop and think about it, life is filled with wonders. The fact that humans have the ability to invent, to create, to communicate and to reach higher levels of consciousness is simply wonderful. All forms of life found on earth, living interdependently with one another, are simply wonderful. The spontaneity and innocence of children is wonderful. The deep affection we feel for our pets and for all living creatures is wonderful. The beauty of the sky, the clouds, the mountains and the setting sun is wonderful. Poetry, painting, sculpture and architecture are wonderful. We live in a world filled with wonders. We need only open our eyes to see them.

Today, I am moved by the wonders that I discover around me. I am in a state of wonderment that brings me closer to my spiritual essence and to God.

FAITH

"Faith is the bird that sings when the dawn is still dark."

— RABINDRANATH TAGORE

*W*e often hear that faith is blind. We believe even though we have not seen. But we can go further to describe the power of faith. Faith is the deep feeling that something is true beyond all appearances, beyond all considerations. Faith is a very elevated level of knowledge that is not fuelled by appearances, opinions or material considerations. Faith is the profound and unquestionable knowledge that exercises a profound influence on us and on the universe. For example, people who have faith in their recovery exercise an extremely powerful influence on their physiological condition. They know beyond a doubt that they will recover and in a sense this knowledge immunizes their bodies against illness.

Today, I see that faith is a form of knowledge that goes beyond all considerations.

THE ENEMIES OF SELF-ESTEEM

*S*elf-esteem — the positive perception we have of ourselves — is a crucial thing. Some behaviours foster self-esteem and others hurt it. We know that derogatory comments, dependence on drugs, gambling or alcohol, a lack of goals and objectives in life, can hinder our ability to love ourselves and to succeed. If we truly want to grow, we must shy away from the enemies of self-esteem whenever they appear on our paths. Our well-being and our survival depends on it. The enemies of self-esteem sometimes creep into our lives in a quiet and unnoticed way. We only realize that there is a problem when it is too late. This is why we should always be vigilant and when we see signs, we should react immediately to eliminate the source that can potentially sabotage our well-being and our survival.

Today, I am vigilant and attentive to the behaviors that can hurt my self-esteem. I accept nothing that can harm my self-esteem because I am a valuable person and I want to live my life in peace and harmony.

The Joy Around Me

"Love is the ultimate meaning of all that surrounds us. It is not a mere feeling, it is truth, it is the joy that is at the root of all creation."
— R. Tagore

Today, I look around me and I see the joy in my life. I see the face of God in every flower, in every tree and in every living creature.

SIMPLY ME

"As life goes on it becomes tiring to keep up the character you invented for yourself, and so you relapse into individuality and become more like yourself every day. This is sometimes disconcerting for those around you, but a great relief to the person concerned."

— AGATHA CHRISTIE

*I*n our formative years, we invent a self for ourselves. We invent the person we think will achieve the best results in life. We invent ourselves for different reasons: we want to be loved and accepted, we want to protect ourselves from life's onslaughts; we want to succeed and we respond to the image that other people have of us. As we grow older, the need to maintain this relatively artificial facade disappears. At last, we give ourselves the permission to be less than perfect, less sociable, less "cool". At last, we can speak openly and show our true colours. At last, we can be ourselves.

Today, I have grown beyond the need to be what I think I should be and what I think other people want to see and hear. At last, I am me — simply me.

WORDS THAT CAN MAKE A WORLD OF DIFFERENCE

*W*e know that some words can make a big difference in the lives of the people who share our existence. We can talk about worthless things, or we can talk about things that are truly important. "I love you." "You are important to me." "I am doing this because I love you." "You are the most important person in my life." "Without you, life would have no meaning." "I will be with you forever, my love." "You are truly wonderful." "I am so happy to know you and to share your life." "You have changed my life forever." "I love you more today than when we first met." "I am happy to grow old with you." "You are the only person I have ever been truly in love with."

Today, I say the words that make a world of difference.

OUR INVINCIBLE SUMMER

"In the depths of the winter, I finally learned that within me there lay an invincible summer."
— ALBERT CAMUS

*E*ach of us must find the inner strength that will help us through life's difficult times. Some people are afflicted with a serious illness. Other must cope with the death of a loved one. Still others have the responsibility of bringing up a handicapped child. These people must find the inner strength to go on and to reach beyond the shattering nature of their situation. This inner peace can take various forms: faith in God's love, the conviction that life's trials and tribulations make us better individuals; a profound sense of responsibility and duty; the undeniable love of self and others.

Today, I face life's difficulties by finding my inner strength. This strength is fuelled by the conviction that I can overcome all obstacles. By living one day at a time, I avoid focusing on my future difficulties.

I Am a Role Model

*E*ach person is a role model. Some models exhibit true virtues such as courage, kindness, charity, competence and compassion. Other project attitudes, appearances and behaviours that are less praiseworthy, such as laziness, greed, violence, perversion or indifference. We are all social beings. We interact with other beings that can be influenced. They look at the people around them and they see many role models. They must choose their own models and their own modus vivendi. I can be a positive influence by being a role model who projects positive values.

Today, I understand that I am a role model for those who share my life. Through my attitudes and my behaviour, I try to be a positive influence on others.

LIFE'S FUNDAMENTAL QUESTIONS

*T*he simplest questions are also the most profound. Where do you come from? Where do you live? Where are you going? What do you do?

We are all caught up in the maelstrom of day-to-day life, where one action follows close on the heels of another. We are involved in a daily routine that is the focus of our attention and that makes us forget about many other things. Then, suddenly, a specific event forces us to ask fundamental questions. This event can take a dramatic form, such as the death of a loved one, or it can be banal, such as a chance encounter with a friend we haven't seen in many years. At that precise instant, we are aware of our specific place in the universe. We look and we see where we come from and we see what we have become over time. Such awareness can be decisive in our lives.

Today, I answer my fundamental questions. I am not afraid to ask these questions because I know that the answers I will find will guide me and will further my personal development.

GOD IS MY FRIEND

*S*ome people refer to God, others to the Supreme Being, and still others speak of cosmic energy. But all agree that there is a benevolent force that is the source of all things. This benevolent force knows our heart and our intentions. This benevolent force follows us throughout our lives and greets us when they come to an end. This benevolent force inspires us, gives us courage and supports us in our darker hours. Our ties to this benevolent force are undeniable and indispensable.

Today, I know that God is my friend. He guides me and inspires me each and every day. He lights my path and allows me to experience beauty and joy each and every day. My friend will never abandon me. He will always be with me, at my side, in times of pain and in times of joy.

GROWING IN HEALTH

"Examine your health; and if you are healthy, thank God and accord it the same value as you do your conscience; because health is the second kindness that we mortals are capable of and it is a kindness that no money can buy."

— IZAAK WALTON

W e realize the value of our health only when we are ill. Even small problems such as colds and flus remind us how important good health is. Of course, we cannot eliminate all possibility of illness, but we can listen to our bodies and our emotions to adjust our practices and our habits. The human body needs proper nutrition, sleep and regular rest, physical exercise, and stimulating social and professional activities. If we strive to satisfy these basic needs, we can minimize the chances of falling victim to a serious illness. We can bounce back from our excesses much more easily when we are young. But eventually, the cumulative effect of excess has an impact on our health and our vitality.

Today, I recognize the important of good health. There are things I can do to protect my health and to minimize the chances of falling ill.

A MATERIAL WORLD

"A wise man never loses anything if he has himself."
— MONTAIGNE

*W*hen we look around, we realize that we live in a very materialistic society. We have built huge production, marketing and distribution systems based on consumption. Children learn very quickly that their identity is defined by their clothes and their possessions. People identify so closely with material things, they become almost as commodities themselves. The identification process is so intense and omnipresent, they have difficulty making a distinction between their possessions and themselves. We spend a great deal of time acquiring and maintaining material things and we work to keep what we have and to acquire even more.

Instead of bringing us the joy and security we expect from it, the accumulation of material wealth weighs us down and hinders our freedom of thought and action.

Today, I focus on my spiritual growth and I turn away from society's obsession with material things.

DEMANDING YOUR RIGHTS

"Nobody can give you freedom. Nobody can give you equality or justice or anything. If you're a man, you take it."

— MALCOLM X

*O*ur social structures are not based on equal opportunity, shared wealth, freedom of expression and justice for all. Modern democracies present flagrant structural inequalities. Each day we see how political and economic power is used to favour one group over all others, or one individual over all others. However, despite the system's imperfections, as individuals we can demand that our rights be respected. Fortunately, many groups and individuals have paved the way for us by abolishing discriminatory laws, by creating a climate that fosters freedom of expression and equal opportunities for all. We have the responsibility to maintain these advantages and to reinforce them by ensuring that our rights are respected and by fighting against silence and injustice whenever we encounter it in our daily lives.

Today, I see that ultimately, I am responsible for my fate. If I am to take my own special place in this world, I must demand my rights and I must ensure that they are respected.

HONESTY

"Being honest is being an individual of quality and character. It is showing — through your words and through your behaviors — the truths you believe in, the values that are inherent in your most elevated thoughts, in your clearest visions. When we are honest, others can trust us and we can trust ourselves. We know that what we bring to our relationships is devoid of any false sentiment, lies or impurity."

— DAPHNE ROSE KINGMA

*W*e know when we are being honest and when we are not being honest. We know whether or not we are telling the truth. We know when we are making the best decision, in the best interest, and when we are choosing the easy route. We will be happy in our relationships only when we are loyal to our true selves, to our principles and to our beliefs. Eventually, the small transgressions we commit, the small lies and half-truths that we use to protect ourselves, will cost us our most valuable relationships. By being honest every day and in all circumstances, we can live happily and can enjoy our relationships to the fullest.

Today, I open my heart to life. I am loyal to my principles and to my beliefs. I know that my relationships can grow and move forward if I am honest at all times.

SLEEP

"For the night was not impartial. No, the night loved certain people more than others, served certain people better than others."
— EUDORA WELTY

*W*e all know that sleep is important to our well-being. Sleep is refreshing and crucial to our mental and emotional equilibrium. When we are deprived of sleep for a more or less long period of time, our efficiency and our attention span decreases, we are less cheerful and more easily distracted.

Today, I understand that sleep is vital for my physical, mental and emotional health. I know that when I get the sleep I need, I am taking good care of myself.

THE LOVE THAT HEALS

*L*ove is a state of mind and a feeling. But love is also a force that transforms and that heals. In life, we encounter many kinds of experiences. Some can be particularly painful and can leave lasting scars. Fortunately, love can console and heal us. Its warmth permeates us; love penetrates to our deepest inner self, it inundates us and touches every part of our being. When we are with someone we love, that person's love comforts us and alleviates — or even eliminates — our past hurts. Affinity, love and admiration are the positive forces that eliminate all pain and all tribulations.

Today, I use the curative power of love to relieve the pain of others. When we feel love in our lives, we can overcome all distress and all hurts.

A BLANK PAGE

"Unless you truly want it, in and of itself, life cannot give you joy. Life can only give you time and space. Only you can fill them."
— UNKNOWN AUTHOR

*M*odern psychology has put a strong emphasis on the factors that determine our attitudes, our intelligence, our behaviours and our aptitudes. Economists would have us believe that our life is determined by economic factors, while geneticists claim that our life is determined by our genes. Deep inside, we know that each individual has the power of self-determination. The more we grow, the more we learn to think for ourselves, the more self-determined we become. The level of awareness of each individual is the one and only determinant factor.

Today, I see life as a blank page that has been given to me. I must fill it. Throughout my life, I use the elements that I find along the way and I use others that have been given to me. I create relationships. I develop plans and I seek the truths that will be useful to further my personal development. Today, I feel that the story I am creating is a story of courage and love. I am filling my page with positive experiences and important realizations.

Choosing a Direction

"The truth is not that some individuals have will power and others do not. The truth is that some people are prepared to change and others are not."

— James Gordon

*W*e all move in one direction. At times, we may feel that we have not chosen it ourselves; at times, we feel that circumstances have forced it upon us; nevertheless, there can be no doubt that we move forward in one direction. We must keep in mind that we always have the choice of continuing in the same direction, or changing directions. The furrows in the path we have chosen may seem so deep that we cannot imagine being able to change directions. Understandably, the effort required may seem overwhelming, but the question remains: Do I want to change direction? When the decision is truly taken, we can overcome all obstacles and we can find the energy we need to change.

Today, I see that I can choose my own direction. I am not the victim of the circumstances in my life. I can choose.

OUR OLD FRIENDS

"Just as old wood is best for burning, an old horse for riding, old books for reading and old wines for drinking, old friends are the most valuable."
— L. WRIGHT

*W*e all know that good and loyal friends are rare. People change. Each of us seeks our own development and our own path. Along the way we can lose a friend who has chosen a direction that is different from ours. Fortunately, despite all the changes in our lives and the lives of others, we manage to keep a small number of loyal friends. These friends have known us for a long time, they have seen us grow and change with the years. And despite all these changes, they know us and they love us. They have chosen to share in our personal development and to accept our changes. They have loved us when we have not been lovable. They have visited us when we were sick and alone. They have remembered us no matter what the circumstances and they have chosen to be there during hard times. We know that good and loyal friends are rare. And we thank God that we have a few.

Today, I am happy to have a few good friends. I see that these individuals are part of the true richness in my life.

KEEPING A DIARY

"I write only to discover what I think, what I look at, what I see and what it means. What I want and what I fear."

— JOAN DIDION

*P*erhaps you know people who keep diaries. At the end of each day, they take the time to write down their adventures, their thoughts and their emotions. Keeping a diary can help us put order in our ideas. By pouring over the events and emotions of the day, we can look at our experiences more objectively and we can learn to assimilate them. We can see the good things we have done and the things we could improve on. We can better understand what makes us happy and what worries us.

Today, I will start a diary. By writing about my life each day, I will be better able to see how I have grown.

OPENING THE DOOR TO LOVE

"It is sad to think that a person can spend an entire lifetime without truly knowing love. Opening the door to true love involves a certain number of risks and requires a certain sustained effort. However, there is no pursuit more worthwhile and more real than the pursuit of true love."
— SANDRA ROBINSON

To be involved in a relationship, I have to be accessible. If I live my life as if I were part of a movie, without really investing myself in it, or if I build an insurmountable wall around myself, I will never enjoy the fruits of love and intimacy. Vulnerability, accessibility and honest communication involve a certain amount of risk. When I make myself accessible, I can be hurt. But without the creative experience of love and friendship, life has no meaning.

Today, I open the door to love and I am accessible to others. Of course, I may be hurt, but I may also experience something real and I may experience a profound and positive transformation.

AN INSTRUMENT OF PEACE

"Lord, make me an instrument of Your peace..."
— SAINT FRANCIS OF ASSISI

S ociety should belong to people of good will who seek and strive to live in peace. Society should be a safe place for children and families. It should protect the innocent and reward those who do their fair share. Obviously, society sometimes fails to fulfill its mission. We reward abuse. We penalize people who work by introducing unfair taxation. Flagrant injustices discourage many and they resign themselves to the situation and refuse to contribute to the proper functioning of the State.

In such a context, we must redouble our efforts to provide a positive example. We are instruments of peace and justice. If we give up the fight for a better society, the world will fall into darkness and infamy.

Today, I see that I am an instrument of peace and justice. I resolve to do what is right and to respect my moral code in all my dealings with others. I will not give up and I believe that society belongs to people of good will.

PROTECTING OUR REPUTATION

*I*t takes years to build a good reputation. We can destroy it in a few minutes. Our reputation is the image people have of us. We devote a great deal of time and effort to building an image of trustworthiness, competence and reliability. A good reputation is worth its weight in gold. We must protect it and nurture it throughout our lives.

Today, I know the value of a good reputation. I strive to protect it by working honestly and conscientiously. I refuse to give in to the impulse of the moment. I act seriously and responsibly.

THE TRUTH OF THE MOMENT

*W*e can spend our lives rushing towards the future and imagining that joy, true happiness and true love will enter our lives eventually. We find no satisfaction in the present and only the hope of a better life in the future gives a meaning to our existence. However, we can choose to return to the present and to see that most of the things we long for are right before our eyes, here and now.

Today, I seek to live in the present. I can see that my present life is filled with good and beautiful things. I can strive for perfection, but I can also see what I have today, here and now.

A NEW SCHOOL YEAR

*T*he month of September marks the start of a new year. Summer comes to an end and as school starts we get down to the more serious side of life. Everyone is back at work and their regular routine. The air feels cool and crisp. The sun takes on a lovely pale yellow colour and the trees are still at their peak.

$$x = \frac{12 - 2y}{3}$$

Today, I look around me and I see the richness of day-to-day life. I feel the tranquility that comes with the return to my normal routine.

A GRACEFUL HEART

"Gestures of gracefulness reflect the soul at their root and lighten the body that carries them out."
— HERVÉ DESBOIS

*G*raceful individuals bring joy to all those who cross their paths. Gracefulness is often associated with the arts. We use the term graceful to describe a dancer, a sculpture or a painting. Yet the word graceful can also be used to describe a likeable and kind person. Originally, the word meant "someone who shows kindness".

Today, I see that tolerance and gracefulness make it possible for me to work and interact with different kinds of individuals and to show them friendship and respect.

COMPLIMENTS

"Many of us are still victims of the old and depressing myth claiming that too many compliments are a dangerous thing, that they can lead to vanity."

— DAPHNE ROSE KINGMA

Admiration is at the root of compliments. When we admire something, we see its beauty and its charm. It is easy to recognize the superior qualities in the people around us. Why not admire and recognize such qualities in the people we love and who share our lives? When we pay sincere compliments, we show others that we admire them and that we recognize the qualities they have. Compliments do not make people vain. Compliments strengthen our ties of affection and communication.

Today, I see that I can compliment others and I can let them compliment me.

THE FLAME OF CREATIVITY

"To fan the flames of creativity, we must be loyal to our own ideas, regardless of how strange or odd they may seem. We are all creative individuals, all we need do is pay attention to our dreams."

— SUE PATTON THOELE

*E*ach of us has our own reality, perception of things, point of view and way of approaching different situations. Ultimately, this means that creative possibilities are endless. Creativity is not limited to artistic expression. We can be creative on the scientific and technical level, on the social and political level and on the level of human relations. First and foremost, we are creative beings. We can interpret each situation. We can work to adapt our vision of the world to our lifestyle, to our relationships and to our profession. We must not simply accept the prevailing reality, we must let our creative impulse break out into the world.

Today, I see a world of creation and creativity. I can do my share and I can live my own dreams.

GROWING OLD JOYFULLY

*W*e know that most people are afraid of growing old. We are afraid of losing our vitality, our beauty, our material well-being, our health and our happiness. Studies conducted among women show that it is possible to grow old joyfully and successfully. A study conducted by Jean Shinoda Bolen shows that women aged 60 to 70 and living alone were the happiest. Perhaps the crux is focusing on the rich experience typical of seniors rather than the losses suffered along life's way. Reaching retirement age means the opportunity of being free and working at our own pace. Growing older means taking the time to live and to appreciate the things and the people around us. It can also mean that we have the time to take care of ourselves. We can grow old joyfully and gracefully.

Today, I see that I can grow old positively. I concentrate my attention on the rich experience I have acquired and not on the losses associated with advanced age.

THE MEANING OF LIFE

"The events in our life happen successively and their meaning follows a specific order — they weave the long thread of revelation."
— EUDORA WELTY

We often forget that the meaning of the events in our life lies solely in the significance we give to them. Events have no meaning in and of themselves. As proof, consider that two people can give a completely different meaning to the same event. For one person, the fact that the children have left home means new freedom. For another, it means loss and loneliness. Since we ourselves give meaning to events, we can also imagine that our perception can change or shift. As time goes on, the intensity of events diminishes. Simply looking at a situation from a different angle can lead to a totally new analysis and can lead us to draw new conclusions.

Today, I see that I give significance to the events in my life. Since I am the originator of their meaning, there is no doubt that I can change my perception of certain situations to decrease the impact they have on my emotions.

CONQUERING SUFFERING

"The human heart never strays very long from what has hurt it the most. Few of us are prepared to make a return visit to anxiety and worry."
— LILLIAN SMITH

We have all lived through experiences that have left a mark and that still today are a heavy emotional burden, even after many years. How can we believe that we can break free from the grip of suffering? We know that some people manage to surmount suffering, while others cling to the pain of past experiences for a much longer time. Some factors can be determinant in the healing of past hurts: acceptance through forgiveness, time's ability to progressively relieve our pain and the ability to overcome our suffering through determination and conscious decision. We can grow beyond our suffering.

Today, I accept that life includes a certain number of painful experiences. I embrace this pain so that I can grow beyond it.

DEMANDS

"We distinguish the excellent man from the ordinary man by saying that the former places great demands on himself and the latter places none at all."

— JOSÉ ORTEGA Y GASSET

The demands we make on ourselves are a double-edged sword. On the one hand, they can help us change, grow and learn. But when we fail to live up to our own expectations, we can feel dissatisfied and even frustrated. The demands we make on ourselves must reflect our nature, our temperament and our abilities. They should help and not hinder our personal growth. The criteria for self-satisfaction should contribute not only to our professional and social growth, they should contribute to our quality of life.

Today, I strive for excellence and I keep in mind that I must live with myself each and every day.

THE JOY OF EXISTING

"You will become what you know. And when you begin to know all the things that exist, you will become all that they are as a whole, that is to say God — complete freedom and the joy of existing."
— RAMTHA

*L*et us return to our source. Long before the human body, long before the earth, long before the universe, long before all imaginable things, there was Being. Being requires only being and it finds all its joy in existence, pure and simple.

Today, I know that I am a being of light, filled with joy and playfulness. I play among the stars.

INNER KNOWLEDGE

"Over time, I have learned that I must attribute the ultimate importance and the ultimate value to my inner knowledge. I have realized that the greatest truth is that which I come to know through my experiences, my senses and my intelligence. There is no more vital or more obvious truth than the knowledge that comes from within me. I know that I must listen to my inner self, to my feelings and to my perceptions. In this way, I will always be faithful to myself and to my principles."

— HAPPINESS — ONE DAY AT A TIME

Today, I listen to my heart. I know that the answers to all my questions are within me. I can trust my inner wisdom because it does not lie.

OUR PASSAGE

"Instead of approaching islands, I sail on the high seas, hearing only the solitary sound of the heart, similar to the sound of the surf. Nothing dies, it is I who moves further and further away, be assured. The open sea, but not the desert."
— COLETTE

D eath is a difficult subject for many people. They contemplate their own death with a deep anxiety and fear, much like the fear of plunging into the unknown. Others have no fear of death. They see their own death as a passage. The passage to a new life or a new form of life. Fear of the unknown is a normal reaction. And the idea of losing our body and all our material possessions can result in extreme anxiety.

It is also normal to believe that there is life after life. The greatest prophets have confirmed that the death of the physical body is not an end, but a new beginning. And more recently, some scientists have studied the near-death phenomenon and have documented that awareness persists after physical death.

Today, I see that death is a passage to a new beginning.

UNDERSTANDING OTHERS

"Compassion is the ultimate and most meaningful embodiment of emotional maturity. It is through compassion that a person achieves the highest peak and deepest reach in his or her search for self-fulfillment."
— ARNOLD JERSILD

*A*ll of us have our own perceptions. All of us have our own reality. Our duty is to understand and grasp the reality of those around us. The basis of compassion is the ability to understand others and their universe while showing an appreciation for them. Communication can only take place if there is a common reality between two individuals. There may be only a small number of individuals who can understand our reality, but our mission is to understand the reality of each individual in our sphere of existence.

Today, I realize that I have the ability to understand others. When I take the time to listen and understand, I can be compassionate.

SMALL GESTURES

"Almost anything you do will be insignificant, but it is very important that you do it."
— MOHANDAS GANDHI

*W*e carry out a multitude of insignificant actions over the course of a day. From the minute we wake up in the morning until we go back to bed at night, we carry out actions that are necessary, but that have no existential value: brushing our teeth, washing a floor, filling a gas tank, paying a telephone bill, drinking a cup of coffee, folding and hanging up freshly washed clothes. These seemingly insignificant actions are part of a whole and although we do not realize it, they contribute to the cohesion and to the profound meaning of our lives

Today, I take pleasure in all of the small things that contribute to the meaning of my life.

SEEING GOODNESS

"There is nothing as easy as denouncing. It doesn't take much to see that something is wrong, but it takes some eyesight to see what will put it right again."

— WILL ROGERS

*W*e must begin to feel personally concerned with what is going on in our society. Currently, we elect a government and then we complain that they do not govern properly. In the past 30 years, we have tried to solve social problems by spending money collected in the form of taxes. But each of us should recognize that we cannot build a cohesive and prosperous society by taking money from workers and giving it to others. Fewer and fewer people are willing to take part in this type of system. Each of us must become directly involved in our communities and must contribute to their proper functioning.

Today, I look at the world around me and I see that I can do something to help.

BUILDING RESERVES

O ur parents and grandparents understood how important it is to save. They lived through very difficult times when it was often hard to find food and clothing. Their generations were profoundly affected by the hardship and poverty of the Depression and economic recessions. Today, society encourages us to consume today and pay tomorrow. And in the process of accumulating material wealth and amassing personal debt, we sometimes forget how important it is to save and to build a reserve fund.

Life in a relationship can be hard if we're unable to put some money aside and if we have no financial reserves. When we're always down to the last cent, unforeseen events can quickly plunge us into a catastrophic situation. By building a reserve fund, we can protect our relationship against financial disasters. If one partner loses a job, we have funds on hand to tide us over. If we want to undertake new projects, the financial resources we need are available.

Today, I understand the importance of saving so that I can maintain my dignity and ensure my independence in the future.

FEELING GOOD ABOUT OURSELVES

*T*oday, I let the light shine into my heart and I am filled with love and tenderness. This tenderness is for others, but it is also for me. With this love and this tenderness, I embrace myself and I forgive myself for my imperfections and all of the mistakes I may have made, consciously or unconsciously.

Today, I let myself live and I give myself permission to simply feel good. I have done nothing special to deserve feeling good about myself. I simply allow myself to feel good because I am a wonderful person and God wants me to know that I am wonderful.

FILLING OUR NEEDS

*T*oday, all of my needs will be filled. I let the light of my being shine and spread. The unquestionable power of my intentions will bring to me all that I need to grow, to learn and to be happy. I am a being of light and I move naturally toward the goodness and the love of God.

Today, there is no reason in the world to prevent me from filling all of my needs.

NEW BEGINNINGS

*"Vitality shows not only in the ability to persist
but in the ability to start over."*
— F. SCOTT FITZGERALD

*M*odern life is in a state of constant
change. We can expect to change jobs
several times over a lifetime. We will
move from time to time and may even go to a different city or a different country. Marriages that
last a lifetime are increasingly rare and we may
be forced to build a new relationship, to start over
with a new family. More than ever before, we
must face new beginnings.

New beginnings require time, patience
and above all, energy. We must establish new ties
of communication, discover the demands specific
to new situations and, to be successful, we must
be able to handle them and respond to them effectively.

**Today, I see that life is filled with new begin-
nings.**

FLYING HIGH

"We have the choice of flying high in an atmosphere of optimism, enthusiasm and febrility, or we can spend our time depressed and earthbound. Do the attitudes we adopt reflect the purity of the atmosphere or are they congested with the dirty air we breathe at street level? We are all free to adopt our own vision of things. If we do not like what we see, we have the courage and the ability to change it."

— SUE PATTON THOELE

When individuals listen to the voice of the Supreme Being, they reach a higher level of knowledge and awareness. They drink from the very source of discernment, the faculty specific to the realm of the soul. They can look beyond the world's outer appearances, make choices based on wider criteria and focus on nobler goals. The Supreme Being always triumphs because it uses the virtues of the heart, kindness, goodness and compassion.

Today, I choose to fly high. I use my faculties of discernment, compassion and my desire to achieve excellence to guide me and to push me forward. I am a being who believes in virtues and in justice. I am noble and great. Today, I move closer to the Supreme Being in my thoughts and in my actions.

NEVER TOO LATE FOR LOVE

"In truth, luck accounts for one percent of the blessings we receive in life, in work and in love. The other 99 percent is the result of our efforts."
— PETER McWILLIAMS

Today, I recognize that it is never too late for love. I open my heart to love.

EXPERIMENTING WITH MY LIFE

"Change and growth take place when a person has risked himself and dares to become involved in experimenting with his own life."
— HERBERT OTTO

No one gets an owner's manual with instructions on how to live life. During our childhood and our life as young adults, we develop principles that may or may not be useful in the future. We adopt values, attitudes and considerations that should help us in the great adventure of life. We also have our intelligence and our creativity and they help us find the path to happiness. But in the end, there are no magic recipes to guide us to serenity and self-fulfillment. We must use our resources and experiment with life before we can find a definitive modus vivendi.

Today, I know that there are no magic recipes for creating happiness. I must use all of my resources, all of my intelligence and all of my creativity to find the answers I need and want.

LIFE'S ADVENTURE IS OTHERS

"I dreamt that I was dead and that a woman was leading me to my coffin. It was open and I could see my smiling skeleton lying in it. I asked why my skeleton was smiling. She told me it was because it had lived a happy life. So I asked her how we can live a happy life. She answered by treating life as an adventure. I wanted to know more and I asked her, what kind of adventure? She simply answered: People!".

— STEVE MARTIN

The only real adventure on earth is the adventure of human relationships. Without relationships, we are not alive. We need relationships. We are here to discover others and to contribute to their happiness. All else is unimportant. All else is superfluous.

Today, I develop relationships and I invest in them. I see that my relationships with others are my only true wealth.

OBSESSIONS

"The man who never alters his opinion is like standing water, and breeds reptiles of the mind."
— WILLIAM BLAKE

*W*e have all encountered individuals who have developed obsessions. They have developed opinions and considerations that build a solid wall around them. We know beforehand how they will react to new ideas. So we don't dare suggest new approaches, for fear of being turned away abruptly. But we can see that these individuals suffer from a lack of openness. They repeat the same mistakes and constantly come up with the same justifications for their suffering. Furthermore, we sense that behind their wall of obsessions lies an ocean of confusion, misunderstanding and false concepts. Fighting windmills is pointless. These people do not want to change and usually, they are not happy to see that others are progressing and growing.

Today, I keep away from individuals who hide behind the wall of their obsessions.

THE ART OF CONSOLING

"One of the most difficult tasks in the love that we feel as human beings is being called upon to console. Consoling is offering our company, it is joining another person at a time of suffering. Consoling is agreeing to explore the depths of a hurt. It is extending a hand and sharing another person's pain."

— DAPHNE ROSE KINGMA

A love relationship requires that we be present and that we understand our partner. We have to see things from the other person's point of view, identify with them, their aspirations and their motivations, their fears and their disappointments. We need not be sad ourselves to understand and appreciate a loved one's sadness. We need not suffer to understand and support a loved one who is suffering. By simply extending a hand and saying: "I am there for you, my love, to share your joys and your pain," we bring consolation.

Today, I resolve to be there for my loved one, in joy and in sorrow. I am a shoulder. I am a hand. And I am a ladder.

SPREADING JOY

"Joy is a fragrance that we cannot spread on others without spreading a few drops on ourselves."

— RALPH WALDO EMERSON

We can spread joy or we can spread unhappiness. Some people set out to spread unhappiness. When they have a chance to hurt someone, they do. We have all encountered a frustrated office worker, a police officer who has something to prove or a boss who wants to keep employees down. We know what effect these people have on others and on themselves. They make us feel misunderstood, worthless, frustrated and unfairly treated.

Similarly, we have encountered teachers who love and encourage their students, mechanics who willingly do a bit more than they are asked to, at no extra cost, just because they like their customers, or store owners who greet people with a smile and a cheery hello. These people spread joy. They attract loyal customers who become friends.

Today, I spread joy around me.

FATAL PREDICTIONS

"Of all the predications that come true in your culture, the assumption that old age means decline and poor health is the most fatal of all."
— MARILYN FERGUSON

Today, I see that what I believe is determinant. If I believe that with the years, I will lose my enjoyment in life, my enthusiasm and my beauty, my predictions will come true. But if I believe that as I age I will find new vitality, new greatness and new beauty, I will. My beliefs are determinant.

THE FOUNTAIN OF YOUTH

"Beauty is unimportant; a beautiful face will soon change, but a good conscience will always be good."

— THE MARQUISE OF LAMBERT

Today, I no longer fight the inevitable. I know that time has an effect on me and on my body. I will not withstand the effects of time. I know that my true beauty will always surface and that I will always be me, in spite of wrinkles, in spite of gray hair, in spite of changes in my body. Today, I accept that physical beauty is ephemeral but the beauty of the soul is everlasting.

EACH EXPERIENCE IS VALUABLE

"It is not enough to take the steps that will lead to a goal; as it moves us forward, each step in itself must be a goal."

— GOETHE

Today, I am interested in my path. I see that each day brings experiences that contribute to my personal growth. Every event can be used to further my growth. Life brings me lessons that I must learn.

MY STAR

"You will find a star to light your path."
— A MIRACLE COURSE

Today, I have the deep conviction that I am guided. I sense that I am not alone on this path that leads to the discovery of myself and the world around me. I do not know all the subtle and loving forces that light my path, but I sense their light deep within me, guiding me each day."

THE SUNNY SIDE OF CLOUDS

"If cancer can bring any gifts with it, it is lesson of living life to the fullest each day. When you are told that you have cancer, the way in which you perceive life is changed forever. And to conquer cancer, you must adopt a very healthy and sound lifestyle to stop the disease from progressing. It is too bad that we have to suffer such a major shock to begin to take care of ourselves and to appreciate every single moment of every single day."

— JACINTHA C.

*E*ach painful experience brings something positive with it, even if that something may not always be obvious. There is suffering, but there is also a newfound vitality and the ability to overcome adversity. There are a number of paradoxes in the human condition. At times only a brush with death can bring us to truly appreciate life.

Today, I see that behind each gray cloud is a sunny sky.

OCTOBER 1ST

CREATING TIES

"An individual cannot live without ties. He needs exclusive ties, partial ties and temporary ties."
— FRANÇOIS GARAGNON

*H*uman beings naturally seek to create ties. They seek to create ties of communication and mutual help to find protection, stimulation and prosperity. Human beings cannot live without creating ties; if not, they focus only on themselves, finding all the ills of the world. They are bored and they forget the meaning of life. We, who are in search of growth and fulfillment, know that the ties we form and reinforce each day are the basis of our evolution as human beings. We know that there is an unquestionable tie between all beings on this planet. We know that we can build lasting ties and we can nurture them throughout our lifetime.

Today, I build ties. I refuse to give in to the mechanisms that would have me shy away from relationships for fear of being hurt and I agree to enter into relationships. My heart is open to life and I contribute to my own growth and fulfillment.

FEELING THE SUNSHINE

*T*oday, I feel the warm rays of the autumn sun on my skin and it makes me happy. I know that life has slowed its pace since autumn began, so I take time for a stroll and I feel the warm breeze on my face.

Today, I feel autumn's warm breeze on my face.

LETTING GO

"There comes a time when we love with all our heart and when, at last, we abandon ourselves completely. We give all that we can and we leave the rest to the superior power of nature and of the universe."

— RAM DASS AND PAUL GORMAN

S ome experiences must be lived fully and without reserve. Some relationships demand complete investment on our part. Our relationship with the Supreme Being is a total relationship that requires complete honesty. When we give ourselves completely and without reserve, we open the door to a profound experience that inevitably leads to transformation.

Today, I open the door to love. At last, I am present and ready to give myself entirely to important experiences, to intimate relationships and to my relationship with God.

RENEWAL

"In me, there is a place where I live alone; there I find an eternal source of renewal."
— PEARL BUCK

*L*ife demands that we be constantly present. There are the demands of work, our family, our relationships and our social milieu. These demands are endless. But each of us must find mechanisms to unwind and renew ourselves. Some people take long walks, others work in their garden, others meditate and still others turn to painting or crafts. It is crucial to refocus from time to time and to find peace of mind.

Today, I withdraw from the world to find renewal. I seek my inner calm. I am not running away from my responsibilities and the day-to-day demands of life. Instead, I am renewing my energy to take on life's demands with greater peace of mind.

LIVING ON A TIGHTROPE

*N*o one can live on a tightrope, thinking that the slightest wrong move will send him to his death. Relationships should let each person in them live and express themselves freely. However, many people live in fear. They are convinced that if they express themselves freely or choose to do something on their own, they will be reprimanded and rejected. This type of relationship is not a human relationship, but a type of master-slave relationship.

Today, I refuse to live on a tightrope. I must have the chance to express myself and to live freely every day. If I see that my partner is attempting to hinder my power of free choice, I rectify the situation. A loving relationship is based on freedom of choice and freedom of expression.

AUTUMN

"... everything that I had wanted had come to pass, a hot southern summer and time at a southern beach, and a summer love. And now, how very happy I was to see that it was autumn."
— ALICE ADAMS

Today, I embrace autumn and the wind of change it brings with it. Autumn is a time for harvesting. Crops are mature and ready for the taking. I realize that I too am mature and I must live the present fully.

THE QUALITY OF MY RELATIONSHIPS

"Each person claims to be a friend: but fool he who believes it;
Nothing is more common than the name,
Nothing is rarer than the thing itself."
— JEAN DE LA FONTAINE

*T*o a great extent, our quality of life is defined by our relationships. The quality of our relationships can be evaluated by the level of communication, by the fairness in sharing, by the respect and affection they involve. The people who share our lives should be honest and they should want to contribute to our well-being. This is fundamental.

Today, when I see that a relationship, either emotional or professional, does not contribute to my well-being, I must put an immediate end to it.

I AM A LIVING LINK

"We are the living links of a life force that moves about in us and exists in us, that surrounds us, uniting the deepest earth and the furthest stars."
— ALAN CHADWICK

*W*e are moved by a life force that lives within us and that vitalizes our bodies. This life force is infinitely good and infinitely wise. We are this life force and it is us. We are beings of light and greatness. In each of us is this life force, kind and filled with compassion.

Today, I trust the life force that lives within me. I know that my wisdom, my inspiration and my intuition emanate from this life force that lives within me and that links me to all other beings in this universe. I use this wisdom every day. And when this life force leaves my body, I will not be afraid. I know that I will leave with it.

THE LIFE OF JESUS DAY AFTER DAY

"Lift the stone and you will find me, cleave the wood and I am there."

— JESUS OF NAZARETH

You need not be a fervent Christian to realize that the advent of Jesus on earth changed everything. Jesus, a wind of change from the East, filled our lives with hope and taught us that love and kindness are the most precious of virtues. An analysis of his testaments shows that he was familiar with Oriental philosophies and came to illuminate the West with his message of peace and mercy. A religious philosophy is a spiritual practice based on love, respect and the possibility of Redemption for all. For the first time, rich and poor were equal in the eyes of God and in their own eyes.

Today, I think of the life that Jesus lived and I see a man who brought us hope and the possibility of living closer to God.

PERSONAL IMPROVEMENT

"I believe that we can live a better life only by seeking to become better; and we can live a pleasant life only in full awareness of our improvement."

— SOCRATES

*W*hen we exercise a trade, we can easily see the improvement in the quality of our work. We see that with time, we can carry out a given task more efficiently and with more assurance. With experience and practice, we reach a degree of assurance and certitude with regard to our work. Observation, study and practice are the tools that make us masters at our trade.

In the area of personal development, improvements are not always easy to see. However, we do see that our relationships are more positive, we can communicate comfortably and we are generally more sure of ourselves. Life seems like an adventure and we are confident that we can take on obstacles with energy and assurance. We see that our lifestyle is the result of conscious choices.

Today, I see that I am on the road to personal improvement. I choose to live consciously and to make the choices that will help me grow each day.

EACH DAY IS A NEW BEGINNING

*T*oday, I know that each day is a new beginning. Yesterday, I may have argued with someone or I may have experienced a disappointment. But the light of a new day has just appeared and with this new day comes every imaginable kind of possibility. I have learned and I am still learning from my mistakes. I am not perfect, but I am improving each day.

Today, I feel that I am embarking on a new beginning and I see a glorious future ahead of me.

THE COLOURS OF AUTUMN

*T*oday, I am amazed to see the colours and breathe in the smells of autumn. I see trees and bushes that seem to be aflame in red, orange and yellow. Nature seems to be waging its last valiant battle before yielding to winter. Nature is more tranquil, its pace is slower, the air is crisp and I am here. I am here amid the colours, the smells and the feelings of autumn.

Today, I am here and I am calm and serene.

STANDING UP AGAIN

*"Our greatest glory consists not in never falling,
but in rising every time we fall."*
— RALPH WALDO EMERSON

*A*ll those who have fought or are fighting a dependence know that it takes will power, effort and perseverance to break free. There is a period of weaning where dependence still has an extremely powerful grip on us, where the body and the mind try desperately to convince us to go back to our old ways. Then, when the worst physiological effects have passed, we must find a new way to live, to identify ourselves and to behave. The risk of a relapse is still very high since in the short term, we must develop new reflexes and a new lifestyle. And finally, when all the elements are in place to enable us to live a life that is free of dependence, we must always be wary of the circumstances that can plunge us into ambivalence and a false sense of security. The fight against a dependence is a major fight. The risks of a relapse are always present. The important thing is to stay on course, no matter what may happen in our lives.

Today, I understand the power, the force of a negative dependence. I am always vigilant; I do not want to experience the hell of dependence.

FINDING SOMEONE TO LOVE

"Loving is not seeing oneself in another, it is looking in the same direction together."
— ANTOINE DE SAINT-EXUPÉRY

*T*here are all kinds of special formulas regarding love and relationships. Some people say we should find someone who loves us more than we love them. Other say that a relationship is a shared love: we should love the other person as much as they love us. And we sometimes hear that if we love too much, the other person will be driven away and will try to exploit us, since we are too blinded to be objective. All these formulas are exactly that, formulas: vague ideas that have no basis in objective reality. We cannot measure the level of love any person feels and no one can build a relationship on this basis.

To live a passionate relationship, we must feel loved, we must know that we truly love and share a common reality. When these elements are in place, the relationship can grow.

Today, I feel that all of the elements I need for a good relationship are in place. I know that there is enough love between us to keep us together and to give us the energy and vitality we need to continue on our path together.

FORGIVING OURSELVES FIRST

"If you have not forgiven yourself for something, how can you forgive others?"

— DOLORES HUERTA

Today, I accept that I have made mistakes in the past. I accept that I am human and that my motivations have not always been the noblest. Now, I see more clearly how I may have hurt others. I also understand that I must forgive myself if I am to continue to grow. Today, I embrace the sadness and the guilt I feel and I forgive myself for the hurt I may have caused.

EXERCISE

"Exercise itself has physical and emotional bene-
fits. However, if you also adopt a strategy that
involves your mind while you exercise, you can
feel a number of benefits fairly quickly."
— JAMES RIPPE

*M*any people resolve to exercise regularly. However, very few succeed. Exercise requires effort and willpower. We
need discipline to include sports and exercise in
our daily lives.

Many people complain that exercise is
monotonous and boring. They give up because of
lack of interest and stimulation. But some forms
of exercise are more interesting than others: a
walk in the country is more stimulating than a
walk on a treadmill; team sports can be an opportunity to meet interesting people; competitive
sports are very stimulating. The idea is to get fit
while having fun.

**Today, I adopt a fitness program based on
stimulation and enjoyment.**

HELLO

"I have often felt that the very moment when you wake up in the morning is the most wonderful moment of the day."

— MONICA BALDWIN

Today, I embrace the soft light of morning. I take the time to breathe the morning's pure air and I look forward to a day filled with joy and enthusiasm.

OUR ATTITUDES CAN CHANGE

"Human beings, by changing the inner attitudes of their minds, can transform the exterior aspects of their lives."

— WILLIAM JAMES

Today, I understand that I am the person who molds and shapes the world around me. My attitudes are determinant. If I believe that I have a beautiful life and I can develop good relationships, then that in fact is what will happen. When I take a close look, I see that my attitudes are like predictions that must come true. Today, I am in control of my attitudes and I make them positive.

TALKING TO OTHERS

"She never talked to people as if they were strange and hard shells that she had to break to get inside of; she talked to them as if she were already inside the shell. Inside their own shell."
— MARITA BONNER

*W*hen we analyze the question of interpersonal communication, we see that many people try to minimize the risks inherent in honest communication. Communication is the only means we can use to reach others. If there are barriers to communication, we risk not reaching our target and not conveying our message. One way to avoid this problem is to address ourselves directly to the individual, and not to his or her defence mechanisms. Look other people in the eyes, convey your message directly using the appropriate tone of voice and the appropriate speed. If the message fails to get through, repeat it until you are sure that it has been received and understood.

Today, I use my talent to communicate effectively with others.

DESIRES

"We should never lose sight of our desires. They are powerful stimulants for creativity, love and longevity."
— ALEXANDER A. BOGOMOLETZ

*E*ach person has an object of desire. Some want to find a life partner. Others want to head a multinational. Still others want to live in the country, to grow in harmony with nature. We can use our deepest desires as powerful trampolines that propel us forward. Our desires push us to take action. Our desires push us to go out, to explore and to discover.

Today, I see that my desires push me to action.

NEGOTIATING

*L*ife is a perpetual negotiation. Each victory, each gain, each relationship and each thing worth acquiring results in a negotiation. Negotiation is based on the satisfaction of needs that are mutual or complementary between two parties. There is always an element of risk inherent in negotiation, since it inevitably involves inequalities between the two parties. At times, these inequalities are barely perceptible, but they exist nevertheless. Negotiation is not based on the annihilation of the adversary, but on the conviction that each party can emerge a winner. Even when one party has the vast majority of advantages, it must agree to accord a partial victory to the other: the relationship depends on this willingness.

Today, I see that I am a negotiator. Each day, I must negotiate the conditions of my existence. I am involved in relationships with others and I must award victories to them so that we can maintain and strengthen our relations.

I CHOOSE CLOSENESS

"I firmly believe that there are as many ways to love as there are persons on earth and days in the lives of each one."
— MARY S. CALDERONE

*L*oving means wanting to be close to the other person. When we love, we admit that there is a relationship between us and the other person, that there is a form of closeness. This closeness is emotional, not physical. The closer we are, the more intimate and even symbiotic the relationship is. Similarly, the further apart we are, the more secondary the relationship is and the more unimportant the love is.

Today, I accept the closeness of love. I open my heart and my life and I let myself be loved. I agree to take the steps that will bring me closer to my loved one.

FACING LIFE

"Face things, always face things, it is the only way to get through. Face things."
— JOSEPH CONRAD

Today, I dare to see things as they are. I dare to face things and to recognize the truth. I realize that all that is worthwhile in this life is the result of my efforts, of my work and of my ability to see clearly. Today, I am prepared to find my way in life by keeping my two eyes open and by refusing to compromise what is true for me.

OUR WORRIES

"If your worries blind you, you cannot see the beauty of the sunset."
— KRISHNAMURTI

O ur worries can imprison us in fear and anxiety. Worry is a vague fear that prevents us from acting and that leads us to imagine the worst scenarios. We are at the root of our own worries. We cannot control all things. However, we can adopt a more relaxed attitude towards life. An attitude based on the acceptance of the prevailing reality. While we cannot control how events will unfold in our lives, we can control our reactions and our attitudes with regard to the inevitable.

Today, I give up my worries. I need not be afraid of tomorrow. Tomorrow is tomorrow. Today, I am here and I am happy and well.

EMBRACING LIFE

*T*oday, I embrace life. I have the opportunity to live fully and to explore all the possibilities life offers me. Now I understand that life is not a rehearsal or a spectator sport. We can hide behind this idea for a time but sooner or later, we must confront it. By taking a stand now and by choosing to be alive and present, I am creating a wonderful destiny for myself.

Today, I give myself the opportunity to explore all of the possibilities that life offers.

TWO ROADS

"If you must choose between two roads, ask God for an inspiration, an intuition or a decision. Then relax and do not worry. After you have done this for a certain time, you will be surprised to see that very often, the right answers emerge on their own."

— BILL WILSON

Today, I feel that I have a direct line of communication with God. He is my ally and my best advisor. When I am faced with a difficult situation, I ask Him for love and advice. He whispers, but I hear His voice in my heart. It guides me and consoles me. Today, I am not afraid of adversity or doubt because God is in my life.

LIVING ON PAROLE

"I spent four and a half years in prison and I can tell you that it is no fun. Life in prison is very hard and very dangerous. You have to watch your back all the time, there is always someone, somewhere who would love to make your life miserable. During my stay in hell, I swore that I would never come back. I had all the time in the world to understand how I had gotten myself into this kind of situation. I had decided to use all possible means to reach my goal. But the price was much too high. Today, I am back on the right road because I know what the life beyond this one has in store for us. Deep inside, I will always be on parole."

— ANDREW S.

Today, I know that there are no shortcuts to success and material well-being. Today, I know that I must respect the other members of society and that I must adopt a code of ethics that ensures my well-being and that of the people around me.

APPEARANCES

"Things are rarely what they seem to be; skimmed milk can pretend to be cream."
— SIR WILLIAM SCHWENCK GILBERT

*W*hen we are engaged in a process of personal development or if we are in a state of emotional suffering, we look for answers. However, we must be vigilant. Society is filled with shamans, false prophets and gurus. They will tell you that they have found the answers and they can lead you straight to heaven. We should beware of letting ourselves be enticed by such snake charmers. We have at our disposal much sounder resources: our inner wisdom fuelled by the support of our loved ones who respect us, philosophical and religious writings such as the Koran, the Bible, the Tao Tse Ching, the Torah and the Talmud, to name only a few.

Today, I listen to my own inner wisdom. I will not let another person manipulate my thirst for knowledge and inspiration.

GROWING WITH OTHERS

Today, I know that I cannot grow alone. I must include others in my personal journey. In fact, my growth is based on relationships. When I include others in my life and when I share all that I have learned with them, I see that I am fulfilling my mission. For me, growing is creating a bigger place for others. Growing is being there for others, accepting their love and their support.

Today, I include others in my journey of transformation and discovery.

PAMPERING YOURSELF

"When I realized that the children were finally gone for good and I was alone with Bernard, I was filled with a feeling of panic. I felt that my life had no more meaning and I was going around in circles. I wanted to repeat the gestures and the small rituals that had always given a meaning to my life. It took several months before I stopped and began to realize that I could live for myself now. Gradually, the panic and the worry were replaced by a new sense of freedom and personal intimacy. Now I am happy and I know that I deserve to pamper myself."

— LORRAINE P.

Today, I know that I deserve to take care of myself and to pamper myself. I need not spend my days making everyone else happy. I can focus my attention on my own happiness.

A FEW MINUTES OF RELAXATION

*T*oday, I take a few minutes from my day for relaxing. I deserve to pamper myself a bit and to give myself a chance to find my inner calm. I can take a nap to revitalize myself. I can take a leisurely walk to clear my mind. I can take the time to chat awhile with a friend. Life is not an infinite series of actions that lead nowhere. Life is simply made for living.

Today, I take a few minutes from my busy day just to relax.

FOCUSING ON THE IMPORTANT

"Enthusiasm, it would seem, is something that depends just as much on the state of interior things as it does on the state of exterior things and those around us."

— CHARLOTTE BRONTË

*W*e can have all the possessions on earth without being happy or in harmony with ourselves. The material world is a trap. We become convinced that the accumulation of material things leads to self-fulfillment. An entire social structure encourages us to accumulate, to spend and to consume. Of course, we must survive and live in pleasant conditions, but the main source of joy lies in human relations. When man is in equilibrium and communicates with his environment, he tends to grow and prosper.

Today, I see that my joy springs from healthy and open relationships. I see that my well-being is the result of my ability to communicate, to share and to grow with others.

CHANGING DIRECTIONS

"I expect to die, but I don't plan to retire."
— MARGARET MEAD

*M*any people view retirement very negatively. While we describe it as a time of rest, a time to take advantage of freedom and the fruits of our labour, for many retirement means withdrawal from a useful life and a type of preparation for death. We all know that we will die, but no one wants to live with the feeling that he is useless. Even if we must envisage retirement from our official jobs, we can develop a "work plan" for retirement. Some may choose to start a business, others can continue to work as consultants, others still can volunteer within the community. The idea is to stay active and feel useful for as long as possible — work confers on us a sense of vitality and self-esteem.

Today, I see retirement as a change of direction. I do not intend to retire from life, instead, I will redefine my responsibilities and my pace.

SOBRIETY

"Generally, when we feel that we have touched bottom, we sense it emotionally at first. But when we touch bottom, we go through a doorway that opens on a new world, the kingdom of spiritual truth. It is only by groping about in complete darkness that we can emerge into the light."
— SHAKTI GAWAIN

Today, I live a life of sobriety and equilibrium. I have experienced excess, inebriety and degradation. I have experienced loneliness, disappointment and lies. I have experienced poverty and misery. Today, I choose to live a life of awareness and enlightenment.

LAUGHING

*R*ecently, researchers discovered that laughter has a therapeutic effect. It is not easy to deal with illness, failure, fear and confusion with a smile on your face. When we feel burdened, we may not want to laugh. However, we can turn to humour. We can spend time with friends who like to laugh and to make others laugh. We can go out to see a funny movie or we can read a funny book. Humour and laughter expose the lighter side of things and events. As we take time to relax, we can find new way to look at life.

Today, I give myself permission to laugh. Today, I look for humour in my life. By laughing and making other laugh, I feel lighter.

FINISHING A PROJECT

"We are beginning to understand that finishing a major project must naturally be followed by a process of mourning. Something that has demanded the best of you has come to an end. You will miss it."

— ANNE WILSON SCHAEF

*L*ife is composed of cycles. Each cycle has a beginning, a middle and an end. At the beginning of a cycle, we need a great deal of energy and determination to ensure that the project starts and moves in the right direction. Then, when things are in motion, our energy must be used to guide and orient. However, each cycle must come to an end. With the end comes the joy of finishing a project and making a dream come true and the sadness of coming to the end of a particular road.

Today, I know that each cycle has an end. I rejoice in the knowledge that with each end comes a new beginning.

Today, I Rejoice

*T*oday, I rejoice in the person I am. I have had to face many difficulties but all in all, I am happy that I have persevered. I see that life has taught me important lessons and has led me to develop all kinds of skills and resources.

Today, I am stronger and wiser than yesterday and I plan to continue my development on all levels.

TOUCHING THE STARS

"Imagination is the beginning of creation. We imagine what we desire, we want what we imagine and finally, we create what we want."
— GEORGE BERNARD SHAW

Today, I feel that I could touch the stars. I imagine how my life will be tomorrow and I see good things. I see love and serenity. I see relationships rich in sharing and communication. Each day, I see myself grow and I have more and more assurance. I will not move backward because I see a glorious future waiting for me.

GETTING RID OF A FALSE IMAGE

"When I was young, I loved to laugh and make my friends laugh. Of course, I didn't earn the esteem of authority figures and they made me feel that I was not very intelligent. Over the years, I developed a negative image of myself. I perceived myself as less intelligent than others and I felt that my efforts to improve would be treated with contempt and would end in failure. When I met Mark, I had given up on the idea that I could live an interesting life. Mark was a go-getter. He didn't like labels. He was convinced that he could do whatever he wanted in life as long as he worked and was loyal to his ideals. Just from being around him, I began to feel my own perceptions changing. I decided to register for night courses and to get my diploma. Gradually, I let go of the false image I had of myself. Today, I know that I am every bit as brilliant and every bit as capable of succeeding as anyone else is."

— STEPHEN L.

Today, I know that the image I have of myself is determinant. I also know that this image was developed over a long period of time and results partially from the image that others have given me of myself. I also know that I can improve and change the negative image I have of myself. If my image does not reflect my aspirations and if it prevents me from growing, I can change it and I can shed it.

THE MESSENGERS OF LOVE

"Blessed are those who heal us of our disparagement of ourselves. Of all the services one can render to man, I know none more precious."
— WILLIAM HALE WHITE

Today, I am filled with gratitude. I had the invaluable chance to meet people who have loved me in spite of myself. They showed me the road to self-esteem and self-respect. Even when I was down, God always sent me a messenger of happiness to help me understand the power of love. Today, I love myself with more tenderness and more compassion, but things were not always thus. So I am filled with gratitude because I have found self-love again. Now it is my turn to become a messenger of love, an envoy of God.

BEING OR SUBMITTING

"The most powerful principle of growth lies in human choice."

— GEORGE ELIOT

A large number of people live with the false certainty that they are victims; victims of circumstances, events, illness, poverty, social and economic injustice. It is very easy to perceive ourselves as victims and to persuade ourselves that external conditions determine our fate. However, growing means choosing and choosing means accepting the consequences of our choice. The choice is simple: we can choose or we can be victims.

Today, I see that my choices determine the specific circumstances of my life. Ultimately, I am responsible for my happiness.

HEALING WITH LOVE

"Love is the greatest power of healing there is. It is far ahead of the miracles of modern medicine, the magic of ancient remedies, the books that we read, our thoughts and our words, although all these things can have a powerful effect on us."
— DAPHNE ROSE KINGMA

W hen a mother brings hot chicken soup to a sick child, is it the chicken soup that has the healing power on the child, or is it his mother's attention and care? Love is a powerful balm that relieves hurts, makes pain more endurable and gives us the profound motivation to heal. Love is a vital energy that protects us and fills us with strength and vitality.

Today, I find my strength and my courage in love. I readily accept the love shown to me and I love because I know that love can conquer all.

WHY GROW?

"Before setting out on the road, the traveller must have determined interests that the journey can serve."

— GEORGE SANTAYANA

*W*hy would we want to grow? Why would we want to reach beyond our initial limitations? Why would we seek to broaden our vision of the world, learn to forgive, to be more devoted and more patient? The answer to these questions is very simple: there is no more noble pursuit. We are moving toward serenity, happiness and love. We seek truth and we seek to discover who we truly are.

Today, I am undergoing profound change. I know myself more than I did yesterday. And as I grow, my life is transformed into a wonderful adventure.

TAKING CALCULATED RISKS

"Take calculated risks. That is quite different from being rash."

— GEORGE PATTON

*T*aking a calculated risk means taking a risk while knowing that the possibilities of failure are limited. When we embark on a new adventure, we know that it involves inherent risks. However, we can begin by examining the risks and orienting our action in light of them. We take calculated risks every day. Driving a car, taking a train, taking an airplane, falling in love — all are examples of calculated risks. We choose to take them because we consider that the rewards of action are greater than the risk of failure or injury.

Today, I know that I must take risks every day. However, I can feel confident because I know how to evaluate risks and I know how to cope with the consequences of my actions.

THE MAGIC OF THE MOMENT

"If you take a flower in your hand and you truly look at it, for that moment, the flower becomes your world."

— GEORGIA O'KEEFFE

In reality, there is only one moment: the present moment. If we waste it by thinking about tomorrow or yesterday, it evaporates quickly and disappears forever. Why not live this precious moment here and now? We can use our power of concentration to remain in the present moment. When we live in the present moment, everything changes. Obviously, by living in the present we risk being touched directly. Our perceptions are completely awakened and our feelings are receptive. Our relationships are more alive and more stimulating. We can savour our food and enjoy the fragrances around us. We can see the beauty of the world in its present state.

Today, I see that the greatest pleasures in life are those we live in the present moment. And so I resolve to live in the here and now.

I USE MY SENSES

*T*oday, I take pleasure in using my senses. I look, I listen, I feel, I touch and I taste. My senses let me establish a link with the physical world and the subtle world. I listen to my own senses and I obey them. They inform me and they help me know more about the world.

Today, I listen to my own senses.

THE DOMINATION OF LOVE

*U*nder the pretext of love, humans sometimes seek to control and dominate. There are many examples of this form of domination: the husband over his wife; the woman over her partner; parents keeping their children under their thumbs; parents who fall victim to their children's blackmail, etc. Obviously, this is not love, but something much less generous. Love is used as a pretext to hide our weaknesses and our emotional dependencies.

This form of double-messaged relationship is very disturbing: we hear "I love you", but must endure painful experiences. We may come to believe that love must be cruel, controlling and arduous. True love is based on freedom, respect and the sincere desire to contribute to the other's enrichment. I refuse to be controlled or dominated for the sake of love. I refuse the blackmail that love can be withdrawn at any time.

Today, I offer my love unconditionally and I avoid relationships that harm me in the name of love.

LOOKING THROUGH THE WINDOW

*"Just when you begin to feel that you won't know
what to do with your time, you have none left."*
— LISA ALTHER

*W*hen the days grow cold, we often stay inside, in the warmth. Life is more tranquil. We spend the evenings at home, reading, looking at TV, talking on the telephone to friends. Winter is a time of rest and a time for revitalization. During the winter, we can easily keep our distance and stay alone with our thoughts. On the other hand, even if everything seems to have slowed down, there is movement. It is the movement of interior growth. We can assimilate things and draw lasting conclusions. We make plans and we imagine the future that we want to create. All that remains are important relationships, important things and the interaction we have with ourselves.

Today, I embrace the northern wind that cools ardour and seems to slow time. I take this time to embrace my inner self and to warm my soul.

THE MASTER OF TIME

"Go slowly, breathe and smile."
— THICH NHAT HANH

Time is something malleable, over which we can have a determinant influence. Time need not be the master of our lives — after all, it is but a system of measurement. But as we grow older, we feel that to some extent, time becomes our enemy. We feel that time is searching us out, pursuing us and dogging our heels. And we live with the certainty that time will catch up with us sooner or later and at that moment, the end will come.

Time is a system of measurement. It measures the evolution of things in space. Time does not invade us, our notion of time invades us, our fear of death, our fear that we have not loved enough, our fear that we have been unable to make our dreams come true, our confusion and our uncertainty regarding the after life. This is what truly pursues us. Time is only a system of measurement. By controlling our fears, we can master time. By living with the certainty that the being persists, the temporality of things takes on more importance.

Today, I embrace the passage of time as I embrace the seasons. Material things are called upon to perish, but man lives on forever.

OUR PHYSICAL APPEARANCE

"After living several years with the feeling that life was a perpetual battle that I could never win, I realized what was happening to me. I didn't like my physical appearance. This new awareness was a genuine shock for me. I saw how I had fought all my life with this unconscious handicap. I didn't like my physical appearance and I had always refused to admit it. I wished that God had made me more beautiful. I was prisoner of a body that I had not chosen. I asked God to take it back and to give me a new one, one that was more beautiful and more attractive. Then one day I understood that my body wasn't what should change, I had to change. This profound realization changed my life forever more. From then on, my physical appearance lost all importance."

— YVAN D.

Today, I understand how things that I refuse to face can take possession of my being. And when I face these demons, they lose their power over my life.

SAVING MY SOUL

"When I was young I often heard that people (especially Catholics) had a soul. In my child's imagination, in the middle of people's chests I thought that I could see something that looked like a transparent bone. It was the image I had of the soul, at that particular point in my life. When I sinned, my soul (my transparent bone) became black. And when I shared my sins by confessing them, my soul became transparent again. I also understood that my soul came from God and ultimately, it belonged to him. He had been generous enough to lend me a soul and a conscience to guide me.

"Many years later, after a number of experiences and several realizations of a spiritual nature, I realized that my soul was not a possession but a spiritual dimension. Such is the difference between having and being. From the moment I came to this understanding, I felt a ray of light shine through me. At last, I was free from a false notion that had hindered my spiritual growth throughout my life."

— CHARLES P.

Today, I know that I am a spiritual being.

THE RIGHT TO INDIVIDUALITY

*W*e have finally won the right to individuality. When we look around, we see that individuality takes very varied forms, sometimes even extreme ones. In some 30 years, we have gone from conformity to total individuality. This phenomenon has an advantage and a disadvantage: we are finally free to express our individuality and our originality without the fear of being persecuted, but society has lost its fundamental cohesion with regard to behaviour and values. We should keep in mind that individuality, the basis of freedom of expression and personal growth, must be manifested in respect for the rights and freedoms of others.

Today, I am happy to be myself. I want to build deep and lasting relationships and therefore, I will not use my individuality to create insurmountable barriers between others and myself.

FREEDOM TO CREATE

"One of the reason why I don't drink is because I love to know that I'm having fun."
— NANCY ASTOR

*M*aturity brings a sure pleasure: the right to define your own lifestyle. When we are 20, we desperately want to be accepted by others, to be part of the group. At 30, we are definitely part of the group and we begin to define our values and our habits. At 40, our involvement in the group has lost some of its importance and we begin to feel freer to be ourselves and to create a lifestyle that suits us. Maturity lets us live with a certain degree of detachment. Our need for acceptance is not as strong and we can live entirely according to our desires and our convictions.

Today, I am free to live according to my desires and my convictions.

TODAY, I WILL DO MY BEST

*T*oday, I know that perfection does not exist. I can strive for perfection and I can do my best. I can be satisfied with a job well done without the torment of knowing that I could have done even better.

Today, I leave perfection to others and I accept the quality and the intensity of the efforts I can make.

THE MAGIC FORMULA

"We are always in search of the redeeming formula, the crystallizing thought."

— ETTY HILLESUM

Today, I know that there is no magic road that leads to self-realization. There is a work of sustained love based on honesty and perseverance, the courage to overcome obstacles, to move beyond suffering; the conviction that I am not alone, that I can count on the help of God and of certain loyal friends. There are no magic formulas that make suffering disappear and that eliminate some of the many steps to personal development. Growing is becoming more conscious and more capable. It is a road that requires work, patience and endurance.

A QUESTION OF PERSPECTIVE

"Change has a considerable effect on the human spirit. For the fearful person, it is threatening because it means that things can shift. For the optimistic person, it is encouraging because it means that things can improve. For the confident person, it is stimulating because it carries the challenge of making things better."
— KING WHITNEY JR.

Today, I see change from an optimistic point of view. I see that everything changes and that I will not be spared. I may give in to my fears and I may try to resist change, but I know that I will not be happy when I do. However, I can overcome my fears, I can embrace change and orient it. By being completely present and by initiating change, I am master of my own destiny.

A WORK OF LOVE

"Saying something good about yourself is the hardest thing in the world. Some people would rather get undressed."

— NANCY FRIDAY

*T*oday, I recognize that I must accomplish a work of love. The first step is embracing myself and loving myself. I do not see self-love as vanity, but as recognition. I am my best friend, my strongest ally. I can congratulate myself on work well done, I can recognize and compliment my qualities.

Today, I am worthy of esteem and self-love.

CLOSING THE DOOR ON NEGATIVE IDEAS

*T*oday, I refuse to accept negative comments and negative ideas. I see how criticism and negative thoughts can discourage and depress me. So I refuse to let people share them with me, just as I refuse to instigate them.

Today, I close the door on negative thoughts and negative attitudes.

LETTING OTHERS LOVE YOU

"By asking for what you need, you reveal your fragility as a human being and you invite the person you love to share his. The reaction to an expressed request not only gives pleasure to the person whose need is being filled, for the person who is filling it, it brings a feeling of effectiveness and the ability to generate happiness. In such moments, both individuals have the opportunity of sharing their love and their humanity."
— DAPHNE ROSE KINGMA

Vulnerability has not always been seen as a desirable quality. We know that when we are vulnerable, we can be hurt. We expose our limitations and our weaknesses; we can fall victim to another person. This is why many of us have learned not to be vulnerable. However, there is another side to vulnerability: the ability to ask for help and for love and the possibility of receiving. In this sense, vulnerability is similar to openness and receptivity.

Today, I prepare my heart to give and to receive love. I have always found it easier to love than to let myself be loved. I thought that in this way, I could stay in control of the situation. But now I see that this approach does not work. Today, I open the door to others.

THE SOCIAL VENEER

"I have always believed that in times of intense stress, such as four days of holidays can be, the thin veneer of the family unit disappears almost instantaneously and each of us appears in his true light."

— SHIRLEY JACKSON

There are times when we see how thin the social veneer is. In a normal context, people can appear to be completely sociable and likeable. Situations of stress, competition or difficulty tend to melt away masks, exposing real motivations and attitudes. This is why each of us has only a precious few individuals in our circle of intimate friends. Our real friends have shown us their true colours. We have seen them in all kinds of situations and they have succeeded in showing true love and compassion regardless of the circumstances.

Today, I see that relationships are covered with a social veneer. I must be able to gauge those around me in spite of appearances and pretensions.

SWEET ESCAPE

"When black thoughts assail me, nothing helps me more than turning to my books. They quickly captivate me and they dissipate the clouds in my mind."

— MICHEL EYQUEM DE MONTAIGNE

*T*oday, I withdraw to catch my breath and to rest. Snuggled up near a fireplace with soft music in the background, I escape from my thoughts. I can look at old photographs, read a book, watch a movie on television or simply look out the window. These moments of relaxation in my own company are so tranquil and so sweet that I feel as if time is standing still.

Today, I escape, even if only for a few hours.

ANCESTRAL WISDOM

"The past, the present and the future; the history of our ancestors and that of our death; in a single moment, all is written, all is lived."
— LINDA HOGAN

*W*e are more than the sum of our experiences. Potentially, each individual has access to a vast reservoir of wisdom that is broader and more profound than the experience of one lifetime. The access to such wisdom is reserved for free beings who have honed their perceptions and set aside the limitations of superficial observation. They listen to the wisdom that emanates from their inner being. And with this ancestral and divine wisdom, they can create, understand and grow.

Today, I see that I am more than the sum of my experiences. If I want it, I have access to an ancestral and divine wisdom that goes beyond the framework of ordinary life.

REACHING THE AGE OF FIFTY

"At 50, we look back with a certain degree of compassion. Capable of learning the lessons the past has taught us, our spiritual needs — if we have nurtured and preserved them — have led us to seek various sources of satisfaction; a divine recognition or a practice that regularly brings us into contact with them."

— MAUREEN BRADY

Reaching the age of 50 means different things to different people. However, it is an important stage in life for everyone. At 50 years old, our perspectives on the future change. We see more clearly the past we have left behind. Beyond the realization that we have grown older, there is the possibility of looking at life with more compassion and more detachment. We enjoy a new vision. We are both young and old. Strong and fragile. We have no time to lose and we have all the time in the world. We are still in good physical shape but we are aware of the importance of maintaining our health. Finally, we are at the height of our abilities and our possibilities.

Today, I embrace my 50 years. I know that life changes and with time, I will develop new perspectives and new possibilities. Today, I see that 50 is only a beginning.

COMPASSION FOR YOURSELF

"Being capable of compassion for yourself and for others opens the door to divine grace. For a woman, it is all the harder because she has always been taught to be there for others: a child, a friend, a lover, a husband, a parent, all those that need help and are suffering."
— VIRGINIA BEANE RUTTER

Today, I have compassion for myself. I see how I have overcome difficulties and become a nobler and more loving person. Now I can embrace myself in moments of loneliness or distress. I can love myself and I can understand myself when I feel tired of life. I can have compassion for myself because I am my best friend.

A WORK OF LOVE

"Why do strong arms grow tired as they careless-ly lift weights? Digging a vineyard is a more worthy task for men."
— MARCUS VALERIUS MARTIALIS

*W*ork that leads to creation and to self-ful-fillment does not have the same quality as routine work. When we create, we find our energy in a profound and infinite source. The work of creation is a work of love, a work that renews and regenerates us. When I garden, when I create a work of art, when I work to build my own business, I find my energy in my mind and in the depth of my being. Work gives way to the joy of creation and wonderment.

Today, I find my energy in the profound source of inspiration and creation. When I carry out the work of love, I am filled with vitality and joy.

A HEALTHY MIND IN A HEALTHY BODY

"A healthy mind in a healthy body is a short but complete description of a happy state in this world."

— JOHN LOCKE

I ncreasingly, we realize that health and equilibrium are directly linked to our emotions and our attitudes. Thus, it is common to believe that there is a close link between our state of emotional health and our state of physical health, that a number of illnesses are psychosomatically based. In general, we are responsible for our emotional health and equilibrium. However, it is not always easy to maintain a perfect emotional and physical equilibrium. With proper nutrition, sufficient rest, regular exercise and activities designed for relaxation and enjoyment, we can ward off illness. A caring and loving attitude towards ourselves is crucial to health and equilibrium.

Today, I take care of myself. Like a plant that needs water, air, sunshine and nutrients, I have needs that must be filled. By taking good care of myself, I protect my health and I find equilibrium.

THE UNBELIEVABLE LIGHTNESS OF BEING

"When I was a child, I remember that I was carefree, that I played for hours on end. I had no worries. I went from one activity to the next with an unbelievable lightness. I was curious and adventurous. I loved people simply and spontaneously. At the time, in the morning I used to wake up happy and radiant. And when I saw my mother's tender and smiling face, I was filled with love and joy."

— CHARLOTTE L.

Today, I am in contact with the child's joy and spontaneity. The child is being in its pure state. The child is an extroverted and present being who simply loves and participates in life. Today, I see that life as an adult is complex, but in its essence, the being is simple, curious and light.

THROWING AWAY THE KEY

"They were so firmly anchored in their beliefs that the time came when the exact nature of their beliefs was no longer important; they were all based in the same stubbornness."
— LOUISE ERDRICH

O ur beliefs have a determinant influence on our attitudes and our behaviours but more especially, on our way of seeing things. Some beliefs contribute to our well-being, our growth and our survival and they must not be put into question. Thus, believing that we should not trust strangers contributes to our protection and our survival. However, other beliefs limit our ability to grow and to see things as they are. Thus, believing that as we grow old we lose our ability to learn limits our possibilities for growth and prevents us from seeing the reality of things. False beliefs such as this are prisons that limit our possibilities by falsifying our vision of things.

Today, I reject false beliefs that limit my capacity for growth.

DISCOVERING THE ARTIST IN ME

"Art is man's desire to express himself, to make note of the reactions of his personality in the face of the world he lives in."

— AMY LOWELL

*W*e often hear someone say that they have no artistic talent. And when we explore the issue, we see that they tried to draw when they were young, but without much success. But Art, artistic expression and creativity know no boundaries, no predetermined form. We can practise Art in the conventional way, by making music, painting or sculpting, for example. But we can also practise it in a much more unconventional way. First and foremost, Art is a mode of expression and communication based on aesthetics. We can cook, dress, speak, write and eat aesthetically. We can express our artistic talent in all possible and imaginable ways.

Today, I express the artist in me. I know that Art takes many different forms and that I can add something beautiful and true to each thing that I do.

SERVING OTHERS

"Life teaches us that all that is truly worthwhile is doing what we do to serve others."
— LEWIS CARROLL

S uccess is based on exchange. When we give abundantly, we open the door to abundance in our own lives. But when we try to hold back, to keep everything for ourselves, we create a sterile environment in which no life, no love and no exchange can manifest itself. On the other hand, when we are eager to give, we open the door to all kinds of possibilities.

Today, I want to serve others. I see that life is fuller and richer when I give and I am ready to serve others. I am not here for myself alone, but to contribute to the happiness of others. When I help someone, I fulfill my divine mission. When I lend someone a helping hand, I move forward on the road to happiness and serenity.

A MOMENT CAN CHANGE A LIFE

"There are people who mark our lives. Even if it lasts only a moment, we are never the same again. Time has no importance but some moments are important forever."

— FERN BORK

*W*hen we look back on our lives, we realize that some decisions, some encounters and some events have had a determinant effect on our personal growth. These crucial moments have profoundly changed the course of our lives. A few moments to change an entire lifetime! These moments, so precious and so rare, occur or are created by us and are crossroads in our lives.

Today or tomorrow, one of these wonderful moments could occur in my life. And then, I will be faced with an important decision that will mark my existence until it comes to an end. And so I am open to the great moments which are among the many that I will spend here with you.

THE NATURAL CYCLE OF LIFE

"We see ourselves dying, we see that certain passages of our life are closed to us forever. And so?"

— SARAH ORNE JEWETT

S omething in us refuses to die. We know that death is there, all around us. We see death in nature. We see death in our relatives, our friends, our acquaintances and we ourselves draw closer and closer to death. But something in us refuses to die, something in us is afraid of the inevitable end.

Death is there when we change our habits or when we put an end to a relationship. Death is before our eyes throughout our lives. Death is part of the natural cycle of life. Death marks the end and the beginning. It also symbolizes birth, change and transformation.

Today, I am in a state of change. I see that death is part of the natural cycle of life. I am not afraid of death because in this end, there is the seed of a new beginning.

THE COST OF LIVING

*E*ach year, the Holiday Season forces us to spend. We may say that the Holidays are a chance to get closer to our families and to share good times. But it is also a time when we should tighten our purse strings and resolve to spend money wisely. The Holidays have become a commercial celebration and each one of us is caught up in the habit of spending outrageously at this particular time of year. If we live within strict budget considerations or if our financial means are limited, the Holidays can be a rather difficult time. Even though we know that the Holiday Season was conceived to serve our consumer-based society, our awareness does not make it any easier to balance our budgets.

Today, I see how important it is to have a balanced budget. By living within my means, I avoid financial crises and problems. I love to give, but I must stay within the limits of my budget.

BEING WORTHY

"Some gestures are assured of success: respecting others, living with as much dignity as possible, trying with your head and your heart to go 'where no man has gone before'... Is this not our ultimate contribution to the experience of Humanity?"
— NIKKI GIOVANNI

Today, I know that I live with courage and dignity. Each day, I seek to do the right thing, to contribute to the well-being and happiness of others. Each day, I do my best and I seek to learn from my mistakes. I am a person who is worthy of respect, of love and of success.

RESISTANCE

*"Is not life but a series of inconveniences...
always the same damned thing over and over
again!"*

— EDNA SAINT VINCENT MILLAY

*B*ased on appearances, life can seem to be
but a series of inconveniences. Yet there
is nothing repetitive in the possibilities
that each day brings us. It is only when we resist
change and transformation that we stagnate.

Unless we accept the process of change,
we will never feel good about ourselves.

**Today, I have faith in my inner path and I
accept change.**

MATURING — ONE DAY AT A TIME

"Until I have exhausted all the resources of my various talents, cultivated all the seeds that can grow within me and until my harvest of them is complete, I do not want to die."
— KÄTHE KOLLWITZ

*W*e develop daily. With time, we mature. We strive to achieve a level of satisfaction in every important aspect of our lives. When we reach a certain age, we realize that some aspects of our lives bring us satisfaction and others still require work. Growing older means becoming more mature. We learn from our experiences. We try new approaches to obtain better results. We change some aspects of our lives to achieve greater personal satisfaction.

Today, I feel that I have matured. With time and experience, I have become a better person.

FAMILY LIFE

*W*hen we look at the issue of personal success, it is easy to see that achieving it may involve neglecting family life. Our families have undergone tremendous change in the past two decades. Today, we are living with the effects of broken families. Nevertheless, the family remains the main source of joy, a sense of belonging and emotional stability. With the family, we learn to share, to love, to shoulder our responsibilities and to take pleasure in the company of others.

Today, I see that family life is part of my values. I seek to reinforce and to fuel my ties with the members of my family. I want to help, to comfort and to pamper the members of my family. I know that alone, life has no meaning. I seek to build healthy, loving and lasting family ties.

THE RUNGS OF THE LADDER

"The most important thing in this world is not where you are, but the direction you are travelling in."

— OLIVER WENDELL HOLMES

Today, I accept that life is a journey. Along my road, there are several destinations, but my path never ends. I cannot be satisfied with only one accomplishment, whatever it may be. I must use each of my accomplishments as the rungs of a ladder that I can use to climb higher and higher.

THE SECOND HALF OF LIFE

"I firmly believe that the second half of life is better than the first. In fact, first we learn how, then all there is left is harvesting the joy of knowing how to go about the business of life."
— FRANCES LEAR

The first half of life is often filled with turmoil, questioning, conflict and painful decisions. The first half is a phase of learning, discovery and stumbling. During this first part, our emotions are on the very surface and we can experience major disappointments.

The second part of life is gentler and easier. At last, we have proven ourselves and we can begin to enjoy the fruits of our efforts, the lessons life has taught us and our experiences. We know ourselves better and we can learn to accept and even love our imperfections.

Today, I embrace the second part of my life with joy and serenity. Now I know myself better and I have learned to accept myself and to love myself as I am.

MENOPAUSE

"When we arrive at this crucial part of our lives, we can only recognize the inexorable progress of life. Without harboring our illusions, without waiting for our permission, menopause calls us to our death. We are consciously aware that we are all mortal, that someday, we will die; but most of the time, for most of us, this is but an abstract idea."

— CONNIE BATTEN

Some of life's passages are more painful than others. Menopause brings with it a variety of feelings and fears. This is a passage that tells us that we are mortal and that we are entering the last major phase of our lives. It is the strongest indication that we have aged and that we have changed. But menopause can be an extremely powerful spiritual experience that brings us closer to ourselves and that makes us appreciate the truly important things in life.

Today, I embrace menopause because I know that it is an inevitable passage. I may not be filled with joy, but I have the certainty that I have all the strength and all the spiritual and emotional resources I need to change this experience into something positive.

AN OPEN DOOR

"When I fell sick and was taken to the hospital, several family members visited me. I was confined to bed and I couldn't escape. I realized how reticent I had been and how I had closed the door on so many people. The realization was almost as difficult and painful as the illness itself. In the end, I was happy to be in contact with my family again. Indeed, there is a positive side to every experience."

— ANNE-MARIE L.

Today, I see that I am not easy to love. In my quest for self-reliance and success, I often forget to let the people who want to love me into my life. Today, I see that I have to open the door.

THERE IS STILL TIME

"It would be really harmful to our well-being, not to say idiotic and disastrous, to believe that because we have arrived at this thankless age that is the age of menopause we are now on the road to the ultimate return. Even if we never reach our ninetieth birthday, menopause nonetheless marks only the halfway point in our lives. Halfway — is it far enough to say that we should give up?"

— MAUREEN BRADY

*W*e must break free from the notion that time is passing and that we have less and less of it left. The freedom of youth is defined by the fact that we feel that we have an eternity of time before us. We can experience new things, take the time to learn and start over. But when we reach middle age, we cannot afford to make mistakes. We must know all and at all costs, must avoid wasting time, the precious time left us. This perception can only limit our growth and our pleasure of living day to day.

Today, I break free from the idea that I no longer have any time to waste. I can live, I can take the time to laugh, to play and to do nothing but enjoy the moment.

COMING BACK TO THE ESSENCE

*T*oday, I celebrate the advent of the light. I see the advent of Jesus on Earth as the advent of a dazzling light that shines in the heart of men and opens the way to true and eternal life. I see that I am not alone in my quest for the light. As the world grows darker, the light of beings becomes more and more visible. Together, we can counter evil and throughout the earth we can shed a new light of love and compassion for others.

Today, I know that I am not alone in my quest for light.

GOD IS AMONG US

"Ritual is the means of feeling the presence of the divine. The ritual is the spark that must never burn out."

— CHRISTINA BALDWIN

T oday, I see the presents and the acts of tenderness and brotherly love. Today, I see that love is among us. Today, I see that God has visited us and has entered our homes to share and to live among us.

Today, I see that we can live in harmony with one another. I think of all beings on earth and I include them in this magnificent celebration of love.

RESPECTING DIFFERENCES

"A man can lead his horse to water, but he cannot force him to drink."

— JOHN HEYWOOD

*I*n virtuous action there is a noble and subtle reality. Forgiveness frees us from evil and past offenses. Compassion opens our eyes to life and each person's individuality. Patience draws us closer to the true nature of things. Kindness, in all its manifestations, gives us the wings of an angel. However, no one can force virtuous action and the desire to do good. Each must choose and see that with this choice comes freedom, dignity and grace.

Today, I accept that all of us must find our own solutions, our own way of being in the world. Today, I respect differences.

THE ANSWER IS WITHIN ME

"We always find what we seek. The answer is always there and if I give it time, it will reveal itself to me."

— THOMAS MERTON

Through prayer or tranquil contemplation, we always end up finding the answers to our questions. When we ask a question, we begin a profound process of interrogation in our souls. The soul, our true being, will seek and will answer. The answer may manifest itself in our dreams, in the unfolding of events or in a profound intuition. We all have a wisdom that is available to us at all times. All we need do is ask and wait patiently for the answer.

Today, through contemplation or prayer, I take the time to collect my thoughts and to see what is truly important for me. I ask God to give me the courage and the strength to overcome barriers and I ask him to show me how to be more loving, more just towards myself and towards others.

IMAGINE

"At that point I thought: it's now or never. Either I stick with whatever is familiar, or I decide to be myself and to be more intrepid. Five days later, I left for Baghdad."

— AGATHA CHRISTIE

*H*ere we are at the edge of a new year. We must decide if the new year will be like all the others, or if it will be the beginning of a new adventure. Adventure already exists in our attitude and in our imagination. We can focus on all that protects us, on all that makes life stable and secure, or we can choose to undertake projects that challenge us and push us to reach beyond our usual limits.

Today, I look toward the future and I imagine the life that I can create. I imagine all the things I can accomplish.

BEING COMPLETE

"In one year, my values changed profoundly. I feel more able to appreciate the pleasure that life offers me, be they intellectual or moral; I sense my wrongs much more easily and more than ever before, I want to be faithful to my responsibilities, to my commitments."

— GEORGE ELIOT

When we begin the second half of our lives, we see more clearly that youth is a preparatory phase. It is a bit surprising to see how youth is glorified in movies, on television and in fashion. There can be no doubt that youth reflects freshness, physical beauty and purity, but it also reflects confusion, immaturity and uncertainty. As we begin the second major phase of our lives, we know that we have gained certainty. We know ourselves better and we know that we can rely on ourselves. On many levels, we are complete, more autonomous and more sure of ourselves. We are aware of our aptitudes, we are capable, determined and in better control of our lives.

Today, I see that I am more whole and more sure of myself.

I PREPARE MY HEART FOR THE NEWS

"You shall know truth and the truth shall set you free."

— JOHN 8:32

*T*here is one sure value in this universe: the power of truth. Truth constantly seeks to manifest itself since in and of itself, it is the highest manifestation of conscience and spirituality. But on earth, the truth can be rare. We must be extremely determined and vigilant to detect the truth in things and events. It is as if this universe we share was based on an enormous lie and through its courage, its work and its intelligence, the soul must find its path to truth.

When we look back on the year gone by to assess it, we must be brutally honest with ourselves. Did we reach our major objectives? Are we happier than we were a year ago? Have we grown in the right direction? Have we made the efforts needed to free ourselves of the excess baggage that slows our personal development? The answers to these questions can help us plan the new year.

Today, I take an honest look at the current situation and I begin the new year with an effective plan of action.

NEW YEAR'S RESOLUTIONS

*M*any people make resolutions for the new year. They seek to make decisions to put an end to old habits, to develop new ones or to achieve objectives that are important to them. Sometimes we succeed in keeping our resolutions, but often soon after the new year begins, we put our good intentions aside and resume our old habits. The reason is simple: the decision or the resolution is in opposition to an older resolution or the powerful force of our habits.

Before making a resolution, we should evaluate the effort needed to break old habits, our level of intention and the true desire to see our resolution achieved. Lastly, it is interesting to determine the circumstances and the motivations that have led us to develop certain habits or behaviours that we now want to change. This small process will help us prepare the groundwork we need to succeed.

Today, I make resolutions for the new year. The resolutions I make will be adapted to my reality and to my desire to change.